# THE AGE OF OPENNESS

D0982286

# THE AGE OF OPENNESS
## China before Mao

Frank Dikötter

University of California Press
Berkeley   Los Angeles

University of California Press, one of the most distinguished university presses in the United States, enriches lives around the world by advancing scholarship in the humanities, social sciences, and natural sciences. Its activities are supported by the UC Press Foundation and by philanthropic contributions from individuals and institutions. For more information, visit www.ucpress.edu.

University of California Press
Berkeley and Los Angeles, California

Published simultaneously outside North America by
Hong Kong University Press
Aberdeen, Hong Kong
www.hkupress.org

Library of Congress Cataloging-in-Publication Data

Dikötter, Frank.
    The age of openness : China before Mao / Frank Dikötter.
        p.    cm.
    Includes bibliographical references and index.
    ISBN 978-0-520-25881-5 (pbk. : alk. paper)
    1. China—History—20th century.    I. Title.    II. Title: China before Mao.

DS774.D55    2009
951.04'2—dc22                                                            2008020954

Manufactured in China

17   16   15   14   13   12   11   10   09
10   9   8   7   6   5   4   3   2   1

# Contents

# Acknowledgements

I am thankful to David Faure for the invitation to contribute to the series *Understanding China:* it provided me with a rare opportunity to sit back and make explicit, in the form of a long essay, some of the more general ideas which have grown out of a series of six more detailed research monographs I have published over the past fifteen years on the globalisation of ideas, institutions and commodities in modern China. A number of people have generously shared their ideas and suggestions with me and read and commented on draft versions, in particular Kingsley Bolton, University of Stockholm; John M. Carroll, University of Hong Kong; Joseph P. McDermott, Cambridge University; Christopher Hutton, University of Hong Kong; Angus Lockyer, School of Oriental and African Studies, University of London; Andrew Nathan, Columbia University; William T. Rowe, Johns Hopkins University; David Strand, Dickinson College; Francesca Tarocco, University of Manchester; and Arthur Waldron, University of Pennsylvania. I bear final responsibility for all errors and omissions.

F. D.
Hong Kong, August 2007

# 1 Introduction

Sir John Plumb, one of the great social historians of the eighteenth century, once said that bland consensus does not do much to advance historical knowledge, and consequently that there is little point in accumulating facts within agreed frameworks of explanation. When we turn to the history of modern China, one of the most pervasive approaches in popular and scholarly accounts written during the Cold War was to take revolution as the key to historical change, so much so that 'revolutionary China' and modern China were often synonymous.[1] 'Opium Wars', 'Unequal Treaties' and 'Peasant Rebellions', seen from such a perspective, are harbingers of decline in the nineteenth century, but the heart of darkness lies between the Sino-Japanese War of 1895 and the Civil War of 1946–1949. An enfeebled Qing is unable to resist the 'carving up' of China by imperialist powers following its defeat in 1895, while a 'Boxer Rebellion' shakes the very foundations of the empire, which soon collapses into chaos. Conventional wisdom has it that after the fall of the Qing in 1911 a weak and corrupt central government dependent on foreign loans is quickly succeeded by a string of rival 'warlords' who bribe, coerce, plot and fight their way to power, as 'China disintegrates'. A measure of political unification, we were told, is achieved by the Nationalist Party (Guomindang) in 1927, but endemic corruption, inept policies, political dissension, continued warfare and economic depression only deepen the country's predicament, popular unrest and peasant immiseration fuelling the success of the Communist Party. Continuous encroachments by imperialist powers culminate in the country's occupation by Japan after 1937, followed by a full-scale war between the Nationalist Party and the Communist Party from 1946 to 1949. 'Liberation' at last closes a sombre chapter in the history of the country, as unification by Mao Zedong brings to an end a long series of humiliations: 'China Has Stood Up'.

Teleology held this approach together. Because so much of the history of the twentieth century seemed to have been about revolution, students tended to look for the 'causes', 'roots', 'stages' and 'origins' of communism.[2] Revolution provided the key for deciding which facts were historically relevant and which were not, a grid through which a unitary understanding of modern China could be created. So entrenched was this approach that even the study of famine, which could potentially have contributed to a critical assessment of the republican era, was neglected: as Sugata Bose has suggested, 'historians of Vietnam and China tend to write more about rebellion and revolution: those of India about fatalism and famines'.[3] 'Imperialism', 'warlords', 'corrupt officials', 'local tyrants', 'peasant immiseration' and 'social disintegration' used to be some of the categories through which historians tried to understand the republican era. As a result, we have a historiography rich on 'exploitation', counterbalanced only recently by work on charity; it is abundant on 'communism', even if work on democracy has steadily been growing; there are gangsters, warlords and prostitutes in abundance, and only gradually are we gaining new insights on polyglot diplomats, returned migrants and businesswomen. And despite many rapid changes in the field of modern history, even today attempts to move away from the conventional wisdom can be met with disapproval: when Fu Zhengyuan devoted an entire book to autocratic politics in China but included four pages on the liberal traditions which appeared before the communist takeover, an otherwise sympathetic reviewer accused him of being 'one-sided' in overlooking the 'dark side' of republican China.[4]

Although variations of this bleak image can still be found in popular accounts, many professional historians have for some time shown that there was far more to the republican era than mere chaos and warfare. Even John K. Fairbank, a proponent of the 'history as revolution' approach, described the period as a republic of paradoxes, as culture, for instance, flourished despite constant warfare. More recent historians such as Parks Coble, Sherman Cochran, William C. Kirby, Mary B. Rankin and Thomas Rawski — to name but a few — have immeasurably enriched our understanding of republican China, while many scholars from Taiwan and the PRC have been approaching the period in a very open way for almost twenty years. A remarkably diverse and cosmopolitan period is increasingly gaining recognition from historians working in fields as diverse as diplomacy and religion. Efforts to document modern China's overwhelming impulse to join the world and open up its borders, minds and markets have been mounting for some time, although we still lack an integrated account illustrating the sheer extent and depth of the country's openness before communism. This book uses a variety of primary sources and a highly informative body of secondary literature to challenge the view that modern China was mainly defined by 'warlords', 'imperialism' or 'disintegration': it suggests instead that in many respects it might very well be qualified as a golden age of engagement with the world. People, things and ideas moved in and out of the republican era, as global flows fostered an unprecedented degree of diversity which has yet to be appreciated in standard history textbooks: globalisation, rather than revolution, appears — with the benefit of hindsight — to have been the driving force of the half-century before the Cold War. The point of this book is not to provide exhaustive evidence for this view, but to avoid bland consensus, provoke critical thought and encourage readers to think creatively: in many cases footnotes refer to detailed research monographs which offer much fuller arguments, while future avenues for research are opened up in all chapters.

Chapter 2 indicates that even if the central government is often believed to have been weak in republican China, it displayed considerable elements of continuity in terms of political vision, administrative practice and government personnel. It also examines the growth of participatory politics and political diversity, from the electorate of 40 million in 1912 to the fully democratic constitution of 1947. It shows how the number of associations and organisations set up independently from the government, from chambers of commerce to beggar unions, increased drastically, and how well over a thousand dailies, weeklies or monthlies circulated already in the 1920s, often published in the treaty ports under the aegis of foreign extraterritoriality. We will see how sustained efforts at legal reform, which included sophisticated legal codification and widespread legal expertise, also contributed to a much more open environment, despite many abuses of judicial independence and judicial administration, which were openly noted and discussed by contemporary critics and government officials alike. Governance, in short, was far more open during the republican period than is usually accepted.

Chapter 3 examines how individuals from all backgrounds, whether ordinary farmers or privileged students, were interested in the world beyond their community, while the opening of the borders led to growing movement of people in and out of the country. Some cultivated distinctly cosmopolitan lifestyles, whether it was the emigrant building a modern house on his return from decades of hard labour overseas, the student publishing in a foreign language after completing graduate work abroad or the diplomat who elected domicile in a foreign concession after years of service in Washington or Geneva. The flow went both ways, and many foreigners did not merely visit China, but made it their home: the second part of this chapter shows how foreign communities were part of the social texture of republican life and should be considered as an integral part of the social history of the country.

Chapter 4 is the most important, and looks at the cultural and social aspects of China's cosmopolitan age. Open borders resulted not only in large flows of people moving in and out of the country, but also in active participation in international conferences and international covenants. Several bilingual lawyers became judges at the International Court of Justice in The Hague, while educated professionals were able to match their foreign peers in many other fields, ranging from avionics to zoology. Ordinary people too were often familiar with the world beyond their community, as illustrated magazines and radio programmes disseminated information about every aspect of the modern world, whether new agricultural techniques or the fluctuating price of silk on the international market. A global outlook was also promoted by the many modern schools which appeared after 1900, as even small establishments deep inside the hinterland introduced their students to the biographies of great foreign figures like Lincoln, Washington, Napoleon, Watt and Edison. Needless to say that a mere handful of students went on to pursue careers as consuls and ambassadors abroad, while only a fraction of the population was fully literate, but opportunities for education were more diverse than ever before, as government organisations, private societies and religious associations, funded by local elites, merchant guilds or foreign benefactors, contributed to the spread of new ideas. Religious expression was also allowed to thrive in a climate of relative tolerance, while culture bloomed in the absence of a monopoly on power and knowledge.

How about the economy? It is not the purpose of Chapter 5 to review all the debates about economic growth in republican China, but merely to underline that economic activities were relatively unhindered in comparison to those closely monitored under imperial and communist regimes. Technological transfers were greatly facilitated by an open society at all levels, whether local workmen building truck bodies to fit imported engines in Beijing or the engineers instructed by Belgian specialists at a cloth-making industry established in distant Lanzhou even before the fall of the empire. The free flow of goods not only transformed the material culture of everyday life (one thinks of rubber galoshes and enamelled washbasins), as a huge range of goods appeared which would not be matched for decades under communism, but it also encouraged the appearance of highly diversified local industries plugged into a much larger global market. The economy was not 'stagnant' or 'regressing' from 1870 to 1930, but steadily growing and thriving, even in the countryside. Human enterprise may have been frustrated by civil war or local officials, but it proliferated even in the hinterland.

Communism and, ironically, nationalism have seen openness as a cause of decline in republican China. However, we now have the critical distance, the archival material and the secondary literature to question this view. While it is certainly true that not all regions benefited equally from the phenomenal changes described in this book, the image of a war-torn, enfeebled if not starving China which comes from the more deprived areas is very much the exception rather than the norm. Whether or not a poor republic is better than a mediocre dictatorship is open to debate, but the diversity of prerevolutionary China surely deserves due recognition. Now that globalisation, rather than 'revolution', has become the guiding issue for the present, from Latin America to India and China, the oft-forgotten cosmopolitan experience of the republican era is of even greater relevance.

# 2  Open Governance

The conventional wisdom sometimes makes two mutually exclusive claims about government in the republican period: first it is portrayed as hopelessly corrupt, fractured and weak, unable to hold the country together, to stand up to imperialist aggression and to provide a measure of stability; second, it is described as oppressive, militarist if not outright fascist, ruthlessly exploiting a weak peasantry, seizing private property, damaging trade, manipulating the currency and silencing opposition. Both views attempt to interpret the era in terms of the communist takeover in 1949. By contrast this chapter indicates that while the central government was relatively weak throughout the republican period, nonetheless significant continuities in governance marked the period from 1904 to 1949, whether in terms of political vision, administrative practice or government personnel. In tune with the overall thesis of this book, it is also suggested that open governance, participatory politics and political diversity were far more significant in the decades before 1949 than has usually been accepted. China before communism was not a model republic, as it suffered from government crises open for all to see, but it was politically more democratic than many comparable regimes in Europe at the time or than the People's Republic has been.

## Cumulative Governance

### 'Militarism' and federalism

'Militarism', in particular in the form of 'warlordism', is alleged to have been one of the main forces of political disintegration, not only in what is often referred to as the 'Warlord Period' from 1916 to 1927, but throughout the entire republican era. So widespread is this assumption that the term 'warlordism' is sometimes seen to be synonymous with 'modern China': Yuan Shikai, who governed until 1916, is referred to as the 'first warlord', and Chiang Kai-shek (Jiang Jieshi) as the 'last warlord' before his escape to Taiwan in 1949. Any critical debate should start with an examination of the origins of the term itself, which is less a scholarly category of analysis than a political loaded expression. As Arthur Waldron has demonstrated in a detailed study,[1] not only was the relatively new term 'warlord' heavily influenced by Marxist ideology, as thinkers such as Karl Liebknecht and Rosa Luxemburg linked 'militarism' to 'capitalism', but much of the anti-warlord propaganda used in the 1920s came from the Soviet Union, including the influential cartoons of Boris Efimov. These images, used first by the Nationalist Party to discredit independent provincial governors during the Northern Expedition started in 1924, were appropriated in turn by communist sympathisers critical of Chiang Kai-shek after he moved against his former allies in 1927: they portrayed him as one of the 'new warlords of the Nationalist Party'. Local artists such as Huang Wenneng contributed popular cartoons linking 'external imperialism' with 'internal warlordism'. These further spread a highly loaded term which presented, in a striking and simple way, the complex and rapidly changing political landscape of the republican era. Sinologists, from Edgar Snow whose influential *Red Star over China* did so much to further communist propaganda, to John K. Fairbank, doyen of Chinese studies in the United States after World War II, found the notion of 'warlordism' congenial, and it has proliferated virtually unopposed to this day.

As Arthur Waldron shows, the term 'warlord' was nonetheless transformed during its voyage from Europe to China, as most commentators in China downplayed the economic determinism explicit in Marxist ideology and instead understood power to come from the barrel of a gun: a strong central force such as a powerful party, rather than class struggle or economic reform, would be able to crush 'warlordism'. A value judgment thus undergirded the use of the term 'warlord', namely that a strong state was desirable, that provincial governors were an impediment to modernisation, and that the entire period was one of 'disintegration'. Faith was expressed in a strong and unified state, while ideas in favour of provincial autonomy within a federal framework were marginalised. Rare were those who, like Hu Shi, a leading intellectual critical of nationalist ideology, understood that disorder did not come from 'warlords' but, on the contrary, from attempts to unify the country by force from above. Hu Shi suggested that in a country as large as China no matter how strong an order imposed from the centre, it would eventually produce division; well-run, self-administered localities, he believed, could knit the country together.

The notion of 'warlordism' has also been used to obfuscate federalist ideas, even if they were popular immediately after 1895 and continued to appeal to a great many scholars and politicians in the first decades of the twentieth century, for instance Sun Yatsen. The republican delegates who by the end of 1911 adopted a constitution for the organisation of a provisional government in Nanjing clearly saw the federal government of the United States as a model to be followed. In the 1920s, the federalist movement emphasised local self-government (*difang zizhi*) as synonymous with government by the people (*minzhi*): it was considered to be a foundation for a lasting federation of self-governing provinces. The constitution promulgated by Hunan province provided for the election of a governor by popular election, and was followed by similar documents in Zhejiang, Guangdong, Yunnan and Sichuan. As Jean Chesneaux commented after studying the federalist movement, 'The American influence is very clear: there was an independent judiciary, and procedures for impeachment and recall were included. Citizens also had the right of initiating laws, Swiss fashion, and of petition before the assemblies.'[2] However, the provincial governors who advocated federalism in good faith have since been dismissed as mere 'warlords', for instance Tan Yankai in Hunan and Lu Yongxiang in the Yangzi valley.[3] Chen Jiongming pursued the creation of a federated state and warned against the tenets of nationalism before attempting to achieve self-government for the province of Guangdong in 1921–22. He was hounded until his death after he was displaced by the Nationalist Party in 1923. With help from the Soviet Union, the party established a military academy in Canton to forcefully unify the country with a 'Northern Expedition', denouncing all its enemies as selfish 'warlords' and portraying federalism as a mere subterfuge used by power-hungry militarists. Chiang Kai-shek's revolutionary army, equipped and trained by the Soviet Union, swept aside federalist forces during the Northern Expedition and by 1926 provincial constitutions, provincial and local assemblies, and local self-government societies and activities associated with the vision of a federated state were no longer encouraged.[4]

However, not all of these political debates and constitutional movements supported the federal integration of the province into a national structure. In Zhejiang province, the dominant trend among politicians, merchants, professional groups and rural notables was to support provincial autonomy: the movement for constitutional autonomy was *a*-nationalistic, committed neither to nation nor to federation but to local independence,[5] not unlike Taiwan today. As Keith Schoppa has suggested, 'provincialism as an integral, functionally positive, and independent outlook' in republican China is often overlooked or portrayed as an 'intermediate stage' towards 'integration'. Here we must mention a related point of historiography: not only was the notion of 'warlordism' used in the republican era to attack autonomous ideals and project a vision of a strong, unitary state, but to this day some history textbooks manage to be both nationalist and imperialist at the same time, never questioning the fact that nationalism in China proposed to unify a territory based on imperial borders. By replicating slogans such as 'the problem of separatism' and 'the need for a unification', some writers imply that the boundaries of the Qing empire were natural and should have been maintained by the republican government. The boundaries of the Qing, reached by imperial expansion during a series of ambitious military campaigns from 1600 to 1880 into the heart of central Eurasia, bringing all of modern Tibet, Xinjiang and Mongolia under the control of Beijing,[6] are roughly similar to the ones claimed, obtained and defended by the People's Republic after

1949. It would be the same if historians upheld the need for a 'strong state' to unify the different parts of what constituted the Austro-Hungarian empire in Europe: it connives in the confusion between nation and empire which lies at the heart of geopolitics in the region referred to as China.

Even if we discard the dubious political values driven by the notion of 'warlordism' and accept that some provincial governors were genuine in their attempts to construct a federalist structure, the question of how strong the military were under 'militarism' still needs to be addressed. We should first puncture the myth that foreign imperialists divided China by selling weapons to local 'warlords', since an arms embargo was enforced precisely by the same powers from 1919 to 1929. The policy, designed to assist the government in Beijing, was abandoned after the Soviet Union started helping the Nationalist Party in building the modern army in Canton with which Chiang Kai-shek unified China in 1926–27.[7] Furthermore, despite the inflated rhetoric about 'swollen armies' and 'chronic warfare', rough approximations made by Thomas Rawski show that military expenditure rose significantly after 1912 but may have reached only 4 percent of total output by the 1930s. That is similar to the spending on military activity during the 1950s of countries such as Pakistan, Australia, Belgium, Thailand and Norway, none of which are usually described as 'highly militarised'. The military in republican China, when compared to its enormous population, was of modest size, the best available statistics showing that in 1933 they occupied less than 2 percent of males between the ages of fifteen and forty-four. One of the most extensive and detailed social surveys of the countryside conducted by John L. Buck confirms that less than one in a hundred rural households reported income from military service. One might hypothesise that farmers did not benefit from the army in terms of income but suffered from its ravages instead. However, besides the fact that armies tended to move alongside the railways and that the economy of areas adjacent to the railways showed substantial increases in farm output, land value and aggregate population,[8] the farmers interviewed by Buck in well over a hundred widely scattered counties did not view warfare as a significant cause of famine: they reported drought as a cause of famine 266 times, flood 127 times and insects 54 times; war was only mentioned 18 times, alongside frost (11) and wind (10).[9]

There are good reasons why the image of large armies bloodying the landscape of republican China is counterfactual. It is true that battles could be fierce: mines, trenches, artillery, armoured trains, naval support and military aircraft were all involved in the war between north and south in 1924, causing such widespread violence and chaos that large sections of the population turned nationalist, helping to propel the Nationalist Party to power in 1927. Warfare and its imponderable, highly contingent outcomes, rather than class or ideology, shaped historical developments in the republican era — as Arthur Waldron has convincingly demonstrated.[10] But financial and geographic limitations nonetheless constrained the size of armies, the quantity and quality of weaponry and the duration of military mobilisation. Thomas Rawski's compilation of casualties during the major wars between 1917 and 1930, to be specific, yields a total of 400,000, a very large number, but one which is nonetheless rather low when compared with other conflicts in China.[11] Why is this number never compared to the 20 to 30 million deaths which were caused by the mid-nineteenth-century rebellions and their imperial suppression, or the many millions killed during movements such as the Great Leap Forward or the Cultural Revolution after 1949? Maybe because it would inevitably lead to the conclusion that attempts to keep a large country unified by force, as happened under empire and communism, is likely to result in high death rates, as Hu Shi argued in his debate in favour of local self-government. It is certain that plundering and banditry were frequent in parts of republican China, as they were in the late Qing, but 'militarism', whether qualitatively appraised by rural residents at the time or quantitatively estimated by historians with the benefit of hindsight, was not a dominant cause of distress.

Military governments, moreover, are not necessarily volatile governments. A number of military figures controlled regions which remained relatively stable for many years, as Thomas Rawski has underscored in his analysis of the lack of substantial negative impact

of the 'warlords' on the overall economy of the republican period
(to which we will turn in much greater detail in the last chapter).
Yan Xishan in Shanxi and Zhang Zuolin in Fengtian, to take but two
examples, established militarily stable and politically strong
governments in which business communities were carefully nurtured:
military finances depended on local prosperity, and heavy taxation
threatened to cut important flows of revenue. Good relations had to
be maintained with powerful merchant communities, who could
demonstrate their strength by boycotts and, more importantly, by
moving out of the region to escape unreasonable financial demands.
In 1927, for instance, the military in Canton was forced to rescind
tax increases by the Chamber of Commerce and the Bankers' Guild,
who threatened to destroy the paper currency on which the army
depended.[12] The crucial point here is that the administration of most
regions under military command remained in the hands of civilian
elites, including local families, merchant communities and university
graduates. In 1931 more than half of county magistrates had attended
higher institutes of education, including legal or administrative
academies. Five years later, a majority of all high-level provincial and
municipal administrators were university graduates, a third having a
degree from a foreign university: administrators with a military
background were in the minority.[13] At the level of the county and
the municipality, the period from 1914 to 1927 was precisely the one
in which local elites concerned themselves almost exclusively with
building up their local area, since no provincial or national
government competed for their attention: this is the case in Rugao
and Nantong, researched by Lenore Barkan and Qin Shao, but more
generally of many other counties, as water conservancy, education,
road building, electrification, small-scale industry and charity all made
significant strides.[14]

## Dispersed government

Dispersed government is not the same as divided government. As
Harold Quigley astutely commented at the end of the so-called

'Warlord Period' in 1927, 'the country is not divided, but the power of the central government is dispersed'.[15] The example invoked by contemporary observers in support of this view was the administration of justice: central control may have been weak but appeals, it was pointed out, reached the Supreme Court from every province except Guangdong in 1924.[16] The inaccessibility of most archival sources in the mainland until the mid-1980s prevented the testing of Quigley's opinion, and for decades a widespread assumption about weak government in the republican era only produced historical evidence about weak government.

However, we do have a recent study of penal administration, based on extensive research in a large number of provincial and municipal archives. Prisons in republican China suffered from underfunding and overcrowding, and inmates were subjected to a degrading regime of institutional discipline marked by continuous boredom at best and death in custody at worst — a situation which prevails in the prisons of other countries, including Britain and the United States, to this day. Financial restrictions further deflected the goal of prison reform in republican China, which was only one task among many others set by the central government. Local, provincial and central authorities had a whole range of pressing issues to concern them, from universal education to basic health care.

Prison reform in itself was a huge project, but the level of administrative and financial resources needed to implement it did not exist in China, any more than it did in economically advanced countries. If then the various plans proposed by the central government were hampered by these constraints, leading to compromises that strayed from grand plans on paper, many local and regional authorities nonetheless strove to abide by agreed prison rules, and often used local resources, human and financial, when the funds provided by the Ministry of Justice were insufficient. However flawed prison reform may have been, it was marked from 1905 to 1949 by significant continuities in penal principles, administrative practices and judicial personnel. Contrary to the negative image of governance in republican China, archival evidence related to prison reform shows that different municipal, regional, provincial and central governments were keen to demonstrate their respect for modern judicial principles in order to abolish extraterritoriality. They invested significant time, effort and money in the cause of prison reform, while many county magistrates, penal experts, prison directors and government officials embraced the prison with great reforming zeal.[17] As John Fincher observes, 'the disorder of national politics in China during the early Republic was not the same as chaos. Misled by the instability of national cabinets and the short terms of early Republican presidents, many analysts of "warlord politics" have ignored the relative stability of certain of the reformed ministries at the national level and of important municipal governments'.[18]

Administrative unity — and arguably the history of the modern state in China — began with the New Policies initiated by the Qing in the wake of the Boxer Rebellion (1900).[19] These reforms destroyed much of the imperial administration by gradually abolishing the traditional examination system, reforming central administrative structures, drafting legal codes and establishing modern ministries instead of imperial boards, all explicitly on the basis of foreign models of governance. As Roger Thompson has argued, these reforms have been ignored by conventional historiographies which emphasise the importance of 'revolution', even if the New Policies laid the foundations for state building in twentieth-century China.[20] This is the case with the Ministry of Justice, in particular its Bureau for Prisons, as different levels of government, regardless of the degree of political fragmentation, closely interacted with each other: county and provincial administrators continued to pursue prison reform from 1905 to 1949 within the administrative framework and penal philosophy created by the New Policies. Even at the height of the so-called 'Warlord Period' in 1926, prison reform across the country was impressive enough to result in a positive assessment by a travelling committee of the Commission on Extraterritoriality in China, representing thirteen countries. The committee examined the courts, prisons and detention houses in a number of provinces and was sufficiently satisfied to conclude that extraterritoriality might be abolished by foreign powers provided a number of improvements could be agreed upon.[21]

Recent research, based on archival holdings previously closed to historians, yields a similar picture: the civil institutions that had appeared with the New Policies often remained in place beneath the turbulent surface of military coups and parliamentary politics, and they were surprisingly active throughout the first half of the twentieth century. For instance, although Manchuria was run as a sovereign state by Zhang Zuolin until his death in 1928, he allowed considerable autonomy to the civil government, and some government officials vigorously implemented fiscal and administrative reforms: the penal principles and administrative practices promoted by the Ministry of Justice in Beijing were enforced by the high court in Shenyang. To take another example, government officials in Jiangsu took their lead from the civil government in Beijing until 1927, despite the frequent changes in the balance of power between military factions. While judicial administration was affected by political instability, military confrontations and financial duress, local and provincial authorities in Jiangsu nonetheless endeavoured to build on the movement for prison reform launched since the late Qing. While prisons never fulfilled any of the promised aims, they were run according to the same principles as in the democratic countries of Europe by 1937. World War II would destroy the efforts of several generations of prison reformers, while the communist victory in 1949 was followed by decades of propaganda portraying republican prisons as medieval torture chambers used against exploited farmers and revolutionary leaders.[22]

Much attention has been given to the instability of ministerial tenure, but just below the level of top political appointments there was continuity of personnel, J. B. Condliffe observed in 1932: 'One is apt to forget in reading of wars and rebellions that the vast majority of the administrators and public servants remain quietly on their jobs. Their power increases cumulatively as the years go by and this body of trained civil servants, together with a revenue sufficient to pay them regularly, is no mean element in the establishment of a stable government.'[23] His view is amply confirmed by our study of the Ministry of Justice: to take but one example, Wang Yuanzeng, director of the model prison in Beijing after 1912, was head of the Ministry's

Department of Prisons from 1932 to the end of World War II. The appointment by the Nationalist Party of many other civil servants who had served under previous governments provided for sustained continuity of personnel, and of the prison rules and regulations, the structure of prison administration, the civil service examination system, the classification scheme and the salary scale for prison officers. The very penal principles that had operated since the late Qing were adopted without significant changes.[24]

One might consider the Ministry of Justice to have been exceptional, but other areas of government showed similar success in building up large administrative institutions. While restricted to the period from 1927 to 1940, Julia Strauss's aptly titled *Strong Institutions in Weak Polities* shows how the Sino-Foreign Salt Inspectorate, the Ministry of Finance and the Ministry of Foreign Affairs were far from being corrupt and useless organisations, and instead provided core services to the wider state building project, being surprisingly successful and effective; her research disputes easy slogans about the corruption, patronage and paper-pushing alleged to have debilitated republican government.[25] Elizabeth Remick also focuses on the 'Nanjing Decade', thus neglecting the New Policies and replicating rather than questioning assumptions about the 'Warlord Period', although her use of the tax and finance records in the Tianjin area and in Guangdong province helpfully illustrates how county-level offices grew in importance and effectiveness until the onslaught of war in 1937: local administrators were becoming more successful in implementing central policies even if the central government itself was weak.[26]

## Participatory Politics

To say that government in the republican era was dispersed but not divided, civil more often than military, stable locally if weak centrally, and cumulative rather than fragmented, does not mean that it was necessarily participatory. After all, the 'local tyrants and evil gentry' so familiar in traditional historiography might very well operate in such an environment, curbing the influence of military leaders and the central government all the better to exploit the people. Prasenjit Duara, for one, writes about the 'local bullies and evil landlords' who acquired power as 'state involution' undermined central government, inexorably leading to 'revolution' — all of this on the basis of a study by colonial administrators of six villages under Japanese control in 1940–42.[27] This section shows that while republican governments may not have been leading beacons of participatory politics, a measure of democracy was achieved before 1949 that has yet to be matched by the People's Republic.

## Elections and democracy

The 'revolution as history' framework, unsurprisingly, used to favour the history of revolutionary ideas: anarchist, socialist and communist thinkers have been analysed in great detail, often out of all proportion with their actual importance. In contrast, proponents of human rights, political pluralism, representative institutions and constitutional government have only recently been taken seriously in republican history. Since, furthermore, received knowledge had it that the period from 1927 to 1949 must be understood as a power struggle between the Nationalist Party and the Communist Party, liberal activists belonging to minor parties and independent elites without party affiliation have received scholarly treatment only in the past few decades. Yet, as Edmund Fung has shown, proponents of civil opposition and democratic reform should be considered as a third force distinct from more state-oriented thinkers who have colonised historiography, whether usual suspects such as Yan Fu and Liang Qichao or communist ideologues such as Li Dazhao and Chen Duxiu. Once we start looking at republican history in all its complexity, we discover a minor but significant tradition of liberal opposition which disappeared after 1949.[28]

Democracy did not wait for the arrival of 'revolution' to appear in modern China. The first formally democratic institution was the City Council of the part of Shanghai which was not under foreign rule in the first decade of the twentieth century. As Mark Elvin has shown, the institution was dominated by influential merchants and officials, often well acquainted with foreign ideas, and strikingly modern, with separate executive and legislative branches. It undertook a variety of municipal functions, including the building of roads, removal of garbage, lighting of streets, running of schools and administration of the police and court of justice with elected judges. Elections broadened with time, and by 1907 those who had been resident in the city for more than five years were entitled to vote, provided they paid more than 10 yuan in local taxes annually.[29] The imperial court itself decreed in 1906 that the country needed a constitutional government in which the voice of ordinary people could be heard. In 1909 provincial assemblies were convened in a two-tier process: first an electorate of 1.7 million voters identified local representatives in county elections, and these in turn selected 1643 assemblymen, who duly gathered in October 1909 in provincial capitals. Elections at the subcounty level soon followed, and were much more open: any literate male who paid the equivalent of one silver dollar in annual taxes could take part; there were 5,000 such elected councils by 1911.[30]

Further elections were held after the establishment in 1912 of the Republic of China, Asia's first republic: the electorate expanded to 40 million people, voting for 30,000 electors, who in turn were responsible for selecting members of the National Assembly and the House of Representatives. As John Fincher has observed, republican China in 1912 achieved a popular representation of some 10 percent of the population, a figure not achieved by Japan until 1928 and India until 1935.[31] Democratic elections ended with the assassination of Song Jiaoren and the intervention of Yuan Shikai in 1913–14, but democratic ideas and participatory politics were by now firmly entrenched, a third provincial election being held in 1918 with a smaller electorate of 36 million people.

As we have seen above, provincial constitutions promoted within the federalist movement were often highly democratic, including a provision for the election of a governor by universal suffrage: in the case of Hunan, for instance, the draft constitution was submitted to an Examining Committee representing 75 counties, ratified by the electorate and promulgated in 1922. Recent work by Louise Edwards shows that it granted voting rights to all citizens who were over 21 years in age but prohibited illiterates (*bu shi wenzi zhe*), bankrupts, opium addicts, those deemed to have improper employment and people with mental illness from voting. The Zhejiang Constitution allowed all people over 20 to vote but excluded illiterates, the unemployed and people with mental illness. The Sichuan document made similar exclusions on the basis of mental illness and illiteracy: it identified the ability to read the constitutional text itself as the benchmark literacy standard. While the emphasis on literacy may have excluded a large proportion of the local population, Edwards builds a compelling case in arguing that there was a change in the basic political culture of China during the first half of the last century from an emphasis on literacy as the basis for political rights to a more universal notion whereby education was no longer a key prerequisite.[32] While much has been written about the cultural icons of the 'May Fourth Movement', in particular the radical wing represented by Chen Duxiu, many of the great reviews with large readerships published in Shanghai at the time favoured democratic institutions, for instance the *Dongfang zazhi* (Eastern Miscellany), the *Taipingyang* (Pacific Ocean) and the *Gaizao* (Reconstruction).[33]

Although the wave in favour of local self-government passed in 1923–24, support for human rights and democratic institutions developed effectively as a protest against the authoritarian policies of the Nationalist Party in the following decades. A vocal minority of pro-democracy writers such as Sun Ke (Sun Fo, Sun Yatsen's son), Luo Longji, Zhang Xiruo, Zhang Junmai (Carsun Chang), Zhang Dongsun, Zhou Jingwen and Zou Wenhai advocated parliamentary democracy and participatory politics. Human rights received patronage at the highest level, for instance by Song Qingling, the widow of Sun Yatsen and sister-in-law of Chiang Kai-shek, although the China League for the Protection of Civil Rights she helped establish in 1932 was forced to close down after six months when Yang Quan, one of its members, was assassinated. Minority parties like the Democratic League, founded in 1941, insisted in opposing autocratic rule, as the war with Japan strengthened rather than weakened the democratic forces. Such was the influence of civil opposition that both the Nationalist Party and the Communist Party had to take it seriously throughout the 1940s: liberal opposition maintained a commitment to freedom of thought, speech and the press and favoured a competitive party system well before the prodemocracy movement of the post-Mao era.[34] To ignore this tradition of liberal opposition just because it did not succeed is to judge with hindsight, as Edmund Fund rightly observes.[35] The international credibility of democratic voices in postwar China was such that P. C. Chang (Zhang Pengjun) served as vice-chairman and Chinese delegate to the UN Commission on Human Rights in charge of drafting the Universal Declaration of Human Rights in 1948.

The Nationalist Party itself supported a measure of openness which contrasts with the more authoritarian approach of the communists after 1949. Often brushed aside, for instance, is the fact that from 1929 onwards general elections were held in villages for the election of the village head: most of the villages in the north visited by Sidney Gamble held an election every year or at least once every two or three years, as 'the elective system gave the poorer and more numerous families an opportunity to express themselves politically and to break the long-continued control of the wealthy families'.[36] In some villages the head, after spirited elections were held, changed every year during the years 1929 to 1933 when they were observed by Gamble. Elections were also held for the National People's Convention, as 500 delegates gathered in Nanjing to pass judgment on the government and approve the provisional constitution: even the *North China Herald*, normally critical of the government, believed that the elections were 'remarkably free from any signs of undue influence' in many parts of the country, even if local committees of the ruling party scrutinised the names submitted from the local counties.[37] In Manchuria, for instance, elections were held in 54 of the 58 districts by a total of 165 organisations, as agricultural unions, industrial associations, merchant guilds, educational institutions, professional associations and party organisations elected three delegates each, including a manager of a cotton mill and a university professor. In Beijing there were 102,000 voters, the majority from farmer unions, representing about one-tenth of the population.[38]

A People's Political Council, created by the Nationalist Party in early 1938 'in order to unify national strength; to utilize the best minds of the nation, and to facilitate the formulation and execution of national policies', underwent democratic changes in 1941, as the number of members was increased to 240, out of which 102 were elected members. As one contemporary remarked, elected members made considerable use of their right to receive detailed reports from government officials and to interrogate them and institute investigations on specific issues; criticism was described as 'lively and frank'.[39] While the powers of the People's Political Council were severely limited, since the final choice of members had to be approved by the Supreme National Defense Council, it forced the government to set up one committee after another and became the venue of a vigorous constitutional movement.[40]

In 1935 the government also started preparations to hold elections of deputies to a National Assembly which would adopt the constitution for the republic. The draft constitution was prepared by the Legislative Yuan and promulgated on 5 May 1936 after the suggestions made by constitutional lawyers, public bodies, civic organisations and the public press were incorporated in six revisions. Elections were held in 1936 to organise the National Assembly, although the assemblymen were unable to convene as a result of the outbreak of war in 1937. When it finally assembled in May 1948, in the absence of the Chinese Communist Party and members of the Democratic League, upward of 1400 deputies from all parts of China attended and adopted a constitution which contained an elaborate bill of rights: it was one of the largest representative bodies ever to meet in any country and it exercised its freedom of speech with gusto, voicing all kinds of discontents. It directly affronted Chiang Kai-shek by electing Li Zongren, an influential figure who attracted liberal politicians, as Vice-President.[41] General George C. Marshall, who followed the process closely as a special envoy, concluded that the instrument was 'a democratic constitution'.[42] It provided for protection of liberty, freedom of speech, religion, association and assembly, freedom to choose residence, and secrecy of correspondence, as well as political rights, including the right to vote and to petition the government. 'Were these rights to be given full effect, the 1946 Constitution would be in full conformity with the international covenants as they exist today', writes Thomas E. Greiff, although he notes how the enumerated rights were seriously hemmed in by a series of constitutional provisions that diluted them.[43] Taken as a whole, however, the extent of participatory politics was sufficient to prompt Carl Crow to write by 1944 that China had become 'a nation which will carry the light of democracy to the millions of East Asia'.[44] With hindsight, this may appear rather naive, but Crow was a fluent speaker of Mandarin who had closely followed political developments during thirty years of residence in China. What he could not predict, however, is how a promising if minor liberal tradition would be snuffed out by the outcome of a civil war in 1946–49.

## A modern press

The printing press, as John Fincher suggests, was the instrument of democratic forces least likely to be controlled by central and provincial officials.[45] The reformist and revolutionary press thrived during the late Qing, the structure of national politics in China leaving ample opportunity for readers to have access to writers who urged revolution against the ruling dynasty; over a hundred newspapers were in circulation by 1907. Well over a thousand dailies, weeklies or monthlies appeared after 1911, often published in the treaty ports under the protection of the foreign settlements and under the aegis of foreign extraterritoriality. Many historians have written about the more politically inclined of these publications, from the revolutionary pamphlets such as *The Revolutionary Army* by Zou Rong to iconic magazines such as *New Youth* established by Chen Duxiu, but countless technical and professional periodicals appeared with titles like *The Journal of Mathematics and Science, The Mining*

*Magazine, The Bankers' Weekly, The Railway Association Magazine, The Finance Journal, The Journal of Agriculture and Commerce, The Chinese Druggist, The Chinese Aviation Journal* or *The Chinese Hardware Journal*.[46] Their circulation was facilitated by an efficient postal system: as early as 1908 it received nearly 36 million items of 'newspapers and printed matter' for delivery. These numbers expanded rapidly in the following decades, and by the mid-1930s there were 910 newspapers published in China in sixteen languages including Arabic, Tibetan and Russian, some claiming sales of 150,000 or more. And, as Andrew Nathan notes, many of these were born to serve a cause: most voices were polemical and highly critical of the central government.[47]

These publications were part and parcel of a thriving print culture which sustained democratic debate, many being published by professional associations and voluntary organisations interested in participatory politics.[48] To give but a few examples, human rights, penal policy, the criminal code, the death penalty and administrative reform in general were regularly discussed in a dozen journals on prison reform set up by small associations of prison warders or penological associations. Writing two years after the Nationalist Party came to power, Li Shijie opposed the death penalty in the *Prison Journal*, arguing that Communist Party members like Li Dazhao had been executed by military rather than civil authorities without due respect for the rule of law.[49] Besides these periodicals, government institutions made available large quantities of official statistics and reports, whereas prior to the establishment of a republic in 1912 government publications accessible to the public were restricted to the annual reports of the Chinese Post Office and the annual trade reports of the Chinese Maritime Customs (both under foreign control). All of these, of course, were in Chinese, but the quantity and quality of information in circulation also benefited from a large number of foreign newspapers published in China, starting with the Canton Register as early as 1827. A lively press in several languages appeared, with English publications such as the *China Press* and the *Shanghai Post and Mercury*, and newspapers in Japanese, Russian and French.[50] A significant international flow emerged in the republican era, as foreign journalists freely roamed the country, while local journalists, sometimes educated in the best schools of journalism abroad, quickly profited from an open environment, founding journalism schools and professional societies. Popular writers such as Lin Yutang acquired international fame, while the work of foreign journalists in turn was frequently translated into Chinese.[51]

It goes without saying that politically offensive publications could be closed down and journalists were arrested and executed, although the degree of government interference varied hugely during the republican era. Under the early republic, for instance, many new publications flourished thanks to the decentralisation of power, while publishers in Xi'an were free to criticise Chiang Kai-shek even at the height of censorship under a unified Nationalist Party in 1936, thanks to the patronage of two powerful governors. Stephen MacKinnon is right to point out that freedom of expression during the republican era was limited, but one wonders in which countries between the two world wars the press was entirely free from political influence.[52] In contrast to countries such as Germany and Russia, a large number of publications in China in the 1930s were relatively open thanks to a politically diverse situation in which editors and writers could always find either foreign protection or political patronage, from foreign concessions in Shanghai to cities controlled by regional governors critical of the central government. The *Dagongbao*, China's most important newspaper before 1949, published commentaries which often lambasted Chiang Kai-shek, and advocated press freedom and political opposition.[53] Edgar Snow could not only visit Mao Zedong in Yan'an, but his propaganda piece in favour of the Communist Party was translated and distributed in most parts of the country. Even with censorship, often erratic and inconsistent, the opportunities for political expression outside of the ruling party before 1949 by far exceeded anything even remotely possible under emperor or Mao.

## Corporate associations

Who read these newspapers and journals? As John Fincher emphasises many never circulated in editions of more than a few tens of thousands. Corporate associations, he argues, allowed educators, merchants, artisans and farmers to follow public debates, as readers from these associations spread their knowledge to others through discussions and meetings. These associations continued to provide a place for local politics even after the suppression of deliberative assemblies in 1914.[54] In Shanghai, for instance, factory workers were passionate about politics: 'Almost everybody in the factory reads newspapers', according to a worker of the Xing Xin cotton mill, and those who could not read obtained information from others. One illiterate woman bought a newspaper every day for her son, who would read and explain it to her, as she wanted him 'to understand society and the present political situation'. Even rickshaw pullers kept up with news, one out of two reading newspapers.[55]

Political diversity in republican China was helped by a drastic increase in the number of associations and organisations set up independently from the government, ranging from imposing chambers of commerce to more informal beggar unions. Never before and never after were there so many voluntary organisations operating outside the realm of the state. It is true that after the mid-nineteenth century the autonomy of local elites was enhanced as the central government only provided a minimal administrative presence: local communities were left with a large margin of freedom to govern themselves, scholars and merchants managing an impressive number of municipal projects, ranging from fire brigades and benevolent halls to ferry docks and hydraulic systems.[56] But overt political associations were discouraged and gatherings of more than ten students prohibited. After the defeat of the Qing by Japan in 1895, however, study societies (*xuehui*) founded by modernising elites burgeoned in the urban centres and in the southern provinces. Similar to the *sociétés de pensée* in pre-revolutionary France, they published polemical essays, news translated from the foreign press and educational articles promoting institutional reform and intellectual renewal. By 1909 some 723 study societies pushed for reform,[57] flourishing in the republican era to reach 1,200 in 1946.[58] Other organisations also thrived: dozens of chambers of commerce were established from 1902 onwards, growing to 794 with close to 200,000 members by the end of the empire.[59] Voluntary associations and popular organisations increased even further after the May Fourth Movement in 1919. When a mass meeting was organised in Tianjin, for instance, the committee consisted of representatives of a whole range of diverse if inevitably overlapping organisations: Ten Men Groups, People's Union, Chamber of Commerce, Provincial Assembly, Church National Salvation Society, Fish Merchants' Guild, Anti-Narcotic Society, Wood Workers' Guild, Native Products Investigation Society, Iron Workers' Guild, Paper Merchants' Guild, Water Carriers' Guild, Women's Patriotic Society, Wet Farmers' Guild, Cotton Guild, Christian Church, Spinners and Dyers' Guild, Cantonese Guild, Fujian-Guangdong Guild, People's Industrial Society, Hemp Workers' Guild, Bankers' Guild, Money Merchants' Guild and many others.[60]

Throughout republican cities, social spaces ranging from temple grounds, restaurants, teahouses, parks, brothels and bathhouses to theatres provided congenial environments for political debates: ordinary people with shared interests gathered to protest poor electrical and water service, discuss government politics, and demand better wages. City walls were used as graphic spaces for political messages scrawled in chalk, while leaflets were handed out on the street or thrown from theatre balconies.[61] These informal gatherings often grew into more formally organised unions, societies and associations; they were subject to a host of qualifications, rules and restrictions, but all vigorously defended the right to meet and assemble, often by lobbying high officials, sometimes by confrontational demonstrations. As David Strand has written about Beijing, 'Citizen participation, cast away from the summit of state power by politicians and militarists who bribed and bullied members of parliament and fixed elections, came to rest at the local level, in the politics of communities, groups, and the street.'[62] Some could be more powerful than their national counterparts, for instance in the case of local chambers of commerce, labour federations and student unions, and many tended towards integration into nationwide systems. While there is an extensive record of political activity among ordinary people who were willing to challenge employers, policemen, politicians and military governors, many also recognised the need for state intervention in providing public services, ensuring economic stability and keeping the social peace. Political integration, in short, came from below, as voluntary organisations contributed towards infrastructural enhancement: 'as plants grow toward sunlight, modern Chinese organizations grew toward political authority'.[63]

A proliferation of participatory organisations also appeared at the county level in the republican era. Even if many merged with newly developed state institutions, they too precluded, in the words of Robert Culp, 'a drift to either the pole of control or that of autonomy'. Confirming what was noted above about dispersed governance, Culp shows that economic diversification encouraged a rapid expansion of managerial organisations at the county level, and these often worked within a broad framework proposed by the central government. Local politics, in short, were not limited to either state domination or regional devolution: in Lanqi, for instance, small communities continued to expand their civil activities by building and running schools, thus improving the primary educational facilities outside the control of the state.[64] Elizabeth VanderVen has also demonstrated how in north China hundreds of modern primary schools appeared, as village communities creatively pieced together resources to implement government educational reforms: the state did not provide money for community schools but did assist village communities in settling disputes in their quest for modernity.[65]

International organisations also started to play increasingly important roles in public life after 1911. The Red Cross and the YMCA, for instance, not only performed a range of charitable services which necessitated constant interaction with local communities and central government, but introduced modes of administration which contributed to a politically pluralistic environment.[66] Voluntary associations, from small village committees to large international agencies, enriched the texture of social life, enhanced the provision of social services and contributed to a vibrant civic environment: political devolution did not mean political disintegration but rather political participation, at local, provincial and international levels.

## Judicial reform

It is easy to overlook the enormous changes introduced in the realm of law in the first half of the twentieth century. As Léon Vandermeersch has argued in a seminal article on the meaning of 'law', under the empire a body of imperial rescripts, regulations and stipulations was imposed by a sovereign without any notion of individual liberty: the power of decision was not separated from the power of execution. The problem of a legal relation between the state and the subject never existed under the empire precisely as a result of the absence of positive law, as a moral, ritual and imperial order was pursued by administrative standards which originated in the will of the emperor.[67] Positive law, which guaranteed in principle the rights of each person, was only introduced after 1900. This movement of legal reform started with the New Policies under the late Qing, as a Ministry of Justice was founded, an independent Supreme Court set up, a new system of modern courts created, corporal punishment abolished, a network of modern prisons established, criminal, commercial and civil codes prepared and a constitution drafted. A Company Law was passed in 1904, not much later than the English and German equivalents introduced in the 1860s. After 1911 the independence of judges was theoretically secured, while the administrative and judicial functions were formally separated, the criminal code being generally revised and enforced. A growing body of civil law culminated in the Civil Code of 1929 and a new Criminal Code came into effect in 1935, showing continued commitment to judicial reform inspired closely by foreign models.[68]

Legal reform and judicial independence was pursued at the highest level of government, even under the authoritarian government of Chiang Kai-shek. Ju Zheng, a graduate from Tokyo Law College, had been imprisoned by Chiang in 1930, and his appointment as president of the Judicial Yuan from 1932 to 1948 demonstrated a measure of independence from the Nationalist Party for more than a decade. He pushed for the abolition of extraterritoriality by implementing judicial reform, even if low salaries and party interference frustrated some of his efforts. But at other levels too, the rule of law was highly regarded, whether by internationally respected barristers and lawyers such as Wang Chonghui, head of the Law Codification Committee from 1917–27, by the many foreign-educated judges appointed to the modern courts such as Zheng Tianxi, later a judge at the International Court of Justice in The Hague in 1936–49, or by the numerous judges, magistrates, prison officers and procurators trained in institutes of higher learning abroad or in the dozens of law schools which spread in China after 1906.[69] Many defended the rule of law by publishing in legal journals or participating in voluntary associations, and they were rarely shy in highlighting judicial shortcomings: in a national judiciary conference convened in 1935, at the peak of the Nationalist Party's power, abuses related to prison reform, judicial independence and judicial administration were highlighted in hundreds of proposals for reform, and legal reform continued unabated until the victory of the Communist Party.[70]

As Laszlo Ladany points out, in the years following the establishment of the Nationalist Party in Nanjing 'the best lawyers were summoned to formulate not only the constitution but laws for all branches of legal life where law applied. This was a continuation of the effort begun in the last years of the Ch'ing dynasty and carried on through the turbulence of division in China.'[71] Legal ambiguities and uncertainties did appear, but, as Meredith Gilpatrick has shown in a detailed study on the status of law under the Nationalist Party, they were in most cases the predictable result of rapid social and political change and of the considerable difficulties of translating modern legal terms: 'during the period of Kuomintang control from 1926 to 1946 the categories of legislation were as clear and unambiguous as a very well-trained corps of lawyers and judges could make them.'[72] Republican China may not have achieved the 'rule of law', as widespread discrepancy existed between the theoretical conception of law and its customary practice, but continued legal reform, sophisticated legal codification and widespread legal expertise were part and parcel of the entire era. These advances were very much facilitated by the free movement of people and ideas, as the next two chapters illustrate.

# 3 Open Borders

Browsing through some of the secondary sources on modern China written during the Cold War one gets the impression that only a few privileged individuals, mainly students and merchants, travelled abroad in the republican era, generally to return as 'alienated' or 'rootless cosmopolitans'.[1] Recent scholarship, presented in the first half of this chapter, demonstrates instead how people from all walks of life, across the social divide, were keenly interested in the world beyond their community, and many travelled in and out of the country, acquiring a distinctly global outlook, from the emigrant returning to his village after decades of hard labour in Indonesia, the soldier repatriated from Europe at the end of World War I or the diplomat retiring in a foreign concession after years of service abroad. People moved in and out of republican China, and the traffic went both ways: the second part shows how deeply enmeshed foreign communities were in the social texture of republican life. Too often portrayed in a negative light, they were numerous, influential and often well established in China, contributing to a pluralistic environment from which the republican era benefited.

## 'Chinese'

Travel outside the imperial realm was prohibited, although enforcement was lacklustre: while relatively few left the Qing in the two centuries after its foundation in 1644, millions of males — many constraints existed on the mobility of women and children — left in the mid-nineteenth century with the suppression of the slave trade, working as contract labourers in appalling conditions on the colonial plantations in Latin America and Southeast Asia, the railways in the United States and the mines in South Africa. Only in 1893 were restrictions on immigration abolished and was the right of imperial subjects to emigrate recognised: working men could now bring their family members to join them. By the time the empire collapsed in 1911 at least ten million emigrants lived abroad.[2]

Not all migrants lived in desperate poverty, and some migrant communities had been established well before the rise of bonded labour in the nineteenth century. In Southeast Asia, for instance, many wealthy and successful merchants were recruited by the colonial authorities into a system of headmanships, assuming communal responsibility for local governance, public works and charitable enterprises while developing the indigenous economy as managers of large-scale colonial plantations or mining operations. These merchant families not only welcomed foreign modes of administration but also seized upon the educational facilities offered by colonial regimes, sending their children to Dutch, French or English schools, many becoming bilingual. Whether colonial authorities favoured assimilation, as in the Philippines where Spanish policy ensured that indigenous women who married foreign men remained Catholics and brought up mestizo families, or on the contrary preferred segregation, as in Java where Dutch rule separated migrant communities from native elites, adaptability was a key to the survival and flourishing of sojourners from China. Some migrant communities were exclusively male and centred on the use of popular religious practices to strengthen social bonds and obtain wider recognition, recruiting further reinforcements from their home villages: this form of chain migration ceased to be predominant with the lifting of the ban on immigration in 1893. Family communities, on the other hand, existed before 1893 in regions where migrant men married local wives, for instance the Peranakan in Java and Malacca, making sure that their male descendants retained sufficient mastery of the spoken dialect to sustain links with the China trade.

In all cases adaptability led to cultural diversity, and this diversity did not square easily with the political demands of the modern nation-state, whether in the countries where migrant communities resided or in China. In China, the very term *huaqiao*, 'overseas subjects' or 'overseas Chinese', was introduced by the end of the nineteenth century as part of a call for help from a dynasty in search of wealth and power against foreign powers, enrolling hitherto scattered communities with varying degrees of identification with the empire into a fight for national revival. On the other hand, sojourner communities and migrant individuals became the target of nationalist movements of host countries, from the Chinese Exclusion Act in the United States in 1882 to the Immigration Act in Australia in 1901. A rising tide of nationalism in Southeast Asia contributed to portraying 'overseas Chinese' as a fifth column stubbornly resisting integration with the broader community: the saying that 'once a Chinese, always a Chinese' encapsulated this belief.[3]

An abundance of evidence, however, shows that individuals and communities labelled 'overseas Chinese' varied enormously in their histories and identities: they moved in and out of republican China in a diversity of ways which can easily be overlooked. Ng Lean-Tuck, better known as Wu Lien-teh, was born in Penang in 1879, sent to English schools in the colony and graduated in medicine at Cambridge University with a Queen's Scholarship. He was a foreigner to China, in the sense that he, not unlike Nehru in the case of India, had to 'discover China' and learn the language after he decided to accept an appointment by the British Foreign Office to travel to Manchuria in the winter of 1910 to help fight a plague epidemic. He remained active in China, establishing the Manchurian Plague Prevention Service in 1912 and devoting the next thirty years to building a modern health service, including hospitals, laboratories and research institutes.[4]

Ng Lean-Tuck was hardly alone: Dr Lim Boon Keng, a third-generation Straits-Chinese born in Singapore, educated in medicine at the University of Edinburgh, a member of the British Legislative Council in Singapore, founder of the Straits Chinese British Association, and recipient of the Order of the British Empire in 1918, served as the president of the University of Xiamen (Amoy) from 1921 to 1937. He only learnt Chinese as an adult and never lost his pride in being a 'King's Chinese', although he was passionate about reform in China. These examples are not unique, as many Straits Chinese were directly or indirectly involved with the republic.[5] They were more often than not Peranakans who had taken advantage of the opportunities presented by English education and had filled administrative and civil service posts in Malacca and Singapore: their publicly expressed loyalty to the British Crown made them known as the King's Chinese. They were a truly global community, often trilingual and able to converse with Chinese, Malays and the British, acting as bridgeheads spanning a continent. Their own language was Baba Malay, a dialect of the Malay language with Fujian words which started disappearing with the end of British rule, as nationalism in Singapore and Malaysia inexorably exerted pressure on the Peranakan to assimilate into mainstream 'Chinese' culture and abandon Baba Malay.

The meaning of 'cosmopolitan', as our discussion about the questionable value of the term 'overseas Chinese' indicates, must also allow for the fact that many individuals portrayed as 'Chinese' had little wish to be connected with China and made very different types of global connections. Song Ong Siang (1871–1941) is a good example: a fourth-generation Singaporean whose family came from Malacca, he graduated from Downing College, Cambridge University, trained as a lawyer and advanced local rights as a member of the legislative council in Singapore. Although he was described as the first 'Chinese' to have received a knighthood from the British Empire, he remained detached from all things Chinese, proclaimed his loyalty to the British Empire and remained a lifelong Anglophile who believed that the British had brought prosperity to Singapore.[6] On the other hand, in Southeast Asia's extraordinary mix of people, some migrants only spent a few years away before returning to China. The career of Tan Kah Kee (1874–1961) is telling: born in Xiamen and migrant to Singapore at the age of sixteen, he made a fortune large enough to be known as the Henry Ford of Malaya and contributed vast sums to his native province, including financial support for the establishment of the University of Xiamen in 1921 and its administration till it was taken over by the government in 1937.

So far this section has focused on the travel of relatively privileged migrants, but ordinary farmers also joined a growing flow of movement in and out of the country, often thanks to the steamer. By the 1880s a labourer could travel from Xiamen to Manila for a little over three Chinese dollars, and tens of thousands arrived in and departed from the Fujianese harbour by merchant steamer every year.[7] Many thousands also went to Singapore and Bangkok in the early 1890s, a rush of passengers often being witnessed just after the Chinese New Year.[8] Steamers eased the movement not only of people, but also of the goods studied in the last chapter of this book: before the end of the nineteenth century, local scholars in Canton observed how coolies and maids imported things modern from Hong Kong and were astonished that some had learnt to get by in English, defeating all prejudice about the 'great unwashed'.[9]

Out of the millions of poor workers who left in search of a better life, many returned after the lifting of the imperial ban on migration in 1893. By the 1920s it was not uncommon for foreign travellers in China to encounter ordinary workers who had spent time abroad. Lady Hosie, for instance, spotted several passengers on a steamer who had worked in the French Labour Corps (a contingent of labourers sent to France by Beijing as a contribution to the war effort against Germany and Austria-Hungary): they had a map of Europe spread out on the wooden deck to go over their routes in memory.[10] Since most workers returned to their ancestral villages, even relatively small places could be islands of modernity closely linked to global trends, in particular in the case of immigrant towns. One of the most significant exports of Guangxi province, for instance, were the many emigrants to the Straits Settlements, Java and Sumatra, of whom many regularly remitted money to their native villages.[11] In Guangdong province many people from Taishan emigrated to the United States: on their return they built modern houses, established modern schools and gradually transformed themselves into a 'model county'.[12] Scattered throughout the southern part of Fujian lived a 'numerous class' of comparatively wealthy emigrants who 'live in quasi-Foreign style, and sometimes even in semi-Foreign houses', as a British trade representative reported in 1904. In Xiamen, he added, eight families out of ten had some of their members earning salaries abroad, while many bought comfortable residences in the foreign concession of Gulangyu, a small island opposite the port.[13]

Several decades later a detailed sociological survey was carried out by Chen Da in a number of small villages in Fujian and Guangdong, which further highlighted the changes wrought by returned emigrants hours away from the larger cities.[14] One returned emigrant, described as representative of the middling classes, built himself a three-floored modern house with a balcony.[15] A modern house in the ancestral village was considered the most important tangible evidence of economic success: real estate in the countryside was used to flaunt new wealth, and in south Fujian and east Guangdong the traveller would regularly come across ostentatious mansions called 'foreign houses' (*yangfang*) in villages where economic migrants had returned: all were inspired by European or American houses.[16] Whether Malay velvet caps, Panama hats, radios, orange juice and coffee or modern medicine and sofas, influences from abroad radiated out from the villages of sojourners. Not all migrants, of course, returned to China, and not all of those who made it back were successful: some found it difficult to find work and to readjust themselves to their former environments.[17] It is also important to bear in mind that the number of migrants only represented a small proportion of the total population of China, and that they tended to come from a limited number of villages and counties in coastal provinces. Their remittances, however, averaged US $80–100 million a year between 1929 and 1941 and were considerable enough to offset the country's massive balance of payment deficits.[18]

Hong Kong deserves a special mention in any discussion about migration in and out of China.[19] Where, before 1893 and after 1949, Hong Kong was a major destination for refugees from the mainland, the flow significantly reversed for more than fifty years between these two dates. Ng Choy, known in Mandarin as Wu Tingfang, was born in Singapore in 1842 and educated in English in Hong Kong, where he graduated from St. Paul's College. He was admitted to Lincoln's Inn to study law and became the first Chinese to qualify as a barrister-at-law in 1877. He acted as a legal adviser to leading statesman Li Hongzhang in 1882 and spent the next few decades playing a prominent role in legal reform, railway construction and the establishment of modern schools, including Tianjin University (known as Beiyang College). He served as Minister to the United States, Spain and Peru from 1897 to 1902, and finished his career as Governor of Guangdong province in 1922. Many other local leaders in Hong Kong chose to cross the border and work in the mainland, for instance Wong Shing (Huang Sheng), a student of the Morrison Anglo-Chinese School who had studied in the United States in 1847, many years before the arrival of official students from the mainland. Ho Kai, a brother-in-law of Ng Choy who was educated first at the Central School in Hong Kong before qualifying both as a medical doctor and a barrister-at-law in England, wrote reformist pieces for an English newspaper, the *China Mail*, and collaborated with Hu Liyuan to have his essays rewritten in Chinese and published in Hong Kong and in China.

This generation of British subjects, often educated in English, was very influential: Sir Robert Ho Tung, the most important property-owner in Hong Kong at the time and an internationally known philanthropist, also worked in Canton for a brief period of time while, much more generally, many boys from the Anglo-Chinese schools in Hong Kong were recruited as pupils by the earliest modern government schools in China. The schools in Hong Kong which received government grants were open to students from all backgrounds, and many were predominantly Chinese, although the masters were British. Year after year students from Queen's College obtained top positions in the best colleges in China, from the Peking Customs College to the Tianjin Medical School, often filling up to half of all available places. Their later careers were also oriented towards China: Alumni of Queen's, for instance, went on to assume important positions in the late Qing and in early republican China. The cabinet formed in the First Republic included no less than three ministers who were alumni from Hong Kong schools, including Ng Choy. Others went on to become consul-generals, bankers, directors of railways, managers of mines and modern farms or presidents of modern colleges, bringing with them a bilingual and modern education.[20]

A cosmopolitan outlook and a bilingual background, however, was not confined to Straits Chinese and Hong Kong Chinese. At government level the extent of English was such that in the 1930s the well-travelled and well-connected corporate lawyer Paul D. Cravath noted, while in Nanjing, that 'I have never associated with a group of foreigners whose speech and thought seemed so much like those of a similar group at home. There is certainly no capital in Continental Europe where so many of the members of the government speak English fluently.'[21] As Kingsley Bolton has shown, a thriving indigenous English-language culture developed in the late 1920s and 1930s, although this has been largely forgotten in the literature on this period. Lin Yutang (1895–1976), for instance, was the son of a local Presbyterian minister from Fujian province and studied both Chinese and English during his secondary education. At St. John's University, Shanghai, he read widely on evolutionary theory, anthropology, history and theology, obtaining a doctorate in linguistics in Germany seven years after he graduated. Lin Yutang moved to New York in 1936, writing novels, plays, travel books and translations in English, many popular enough to establish him as the 'Emerson of China' and arguably as the most prolific Chinese writer of English of the twentieth century.[22]

Before Lin moved to the United States, he also contributed numerous articles to two English-language publications, the weekly *China Critic* and the *T'ien Hsia Monthly*. These two influential publications were remarkable in that they were written in English by bilingual Chinese for bilingual Chinese as well as an international readership. Wen Yuanning, a graduate of Cambridge University, was a member of the editorial board of *T'ien Hsia Monthly*, taught at National Peking University and later became an ambassador to Greece. Another member of the group, Wu Jingxiong, or John Wu, underwent postgraduate training at the University of Michigan and was one of the most brilliant members of the *T'ien Hsia* group, becoming a judge in 1927, a member of the Legislative Yuan and the author of the first draft of the new national constitution in 1936

(mentioned in Chapter 2). The then president of the Leg
Yuan, Sun Ke, the son of Sun Yatsen, was also a member of the group,
writing how 'culture has always maintained an Open Door policy.
There is only one condition for entry — the humility to learn.'[23] All
the contributors to the weekly were convinced humanists and
cosmopolitans, while foreigners such as Harold Acton, C. R. Boxer,
Emily Hahn, Herbert Read, Henry Miller and Arthur Waley also
contributed to this spirit with a large number of original essays.

And they were not alone. Many intellectuals in Shanghai fell into
three groups, each with its own educational background, namely the
'English-language group', educated in England, the United States or
universities such as St. John's, Tsinghua and Yenching, the 'French-
German group', often educated at Aurora Catholic University in
Shanghai, and the 'Japanese-language group', including those who
had studied in Japan: all were engaged in a global dialogue premised
on familiarity with the rest of the world. These links also existed far
beyond the intellectual circles of Shanghai, the best example being
the complex relations forged by local children adopted by missionary
families in the hinterland. Jin Yunmei, for instance, was born in
Ningbo, adopted by an American couple, educated in Japan and the
United States and the first 'Chinese' woman to receive a medical
degree in 1885. Mary Stone (Shi Meiyu), despite her name, was a
local girl who studied in the Methodist Girls' School in Jiujiang under
Gertrude Howe. She read medicine at the University of Michigan
where she graduated in 1896. Ida Kahn (Kang Cheng), the adopted
daughter of Gertrude Howe, also received her degree in medicine
from the University of Michigan in 1896. Together with Mary Stone
they established the Danforth Memorial Hospital in Jiujiang on their
return to China the same year.[24]

# 'Foreigners'

Over 350,000 officially registered foreigners resided in China in 1919,
many more probably living in the country's border towns. Traders
from Turkistan, Mongolia, Siberia, Tibet and India could even be met

in the streets of the remote provincial capital of Lanzhou, throbbing with life and energy, far away from the hustle and bustle of coastal metropoles like Shanghai and Tianjin.[25] Eighty years later, on the other hand, a mere 300,000 foreigners were registered among a population accounting for a quarter of humanity, less than the number of refugees from Bosnia resident in Germany in 1995. Such was the importance of foreign communities before 1949 that many European countries maintained a string of consulates, besides their embassies. Germany alone in 1913 staffed one consulate-general and sixteen consulates, while even a small country like the Netherlands had nine, when most large countries nowadays maintain only two, generally in Shanghai and in Canton.[26] Direct flights, despite the expense, existed between the United States, Europe and China: KLM, for instance, was not only the first continental European airline to open transatlantic services to the USA after World War II, but also flew to the Far East, including China, a fact it conveniently ignored when it reopened its route to Shanghai with an 'inaugural' flight in 1999. This striking contrast points to a very simply truth: between 1911 and 1949, borders were open in a way they had never been before.

The increase in the number of foreigners living in China was most marked after the fall of the empire: in 1914, the foreign population was about 165,000, rapidly increasing to 245,000 in 1918 and reaching over 350,000 a year later, half being Japanese, as well as approximately 148,000 Russians, 13,200 British, 6,700 Americans and 4,400 French.[27] These communities had gained a foothold well before the collapse of the empire, as treaty ports such as Shanghai and Tianjin had concessions under foreign administration since the Sino-British Wars of 1839–42 and 1858–60. Foreign residents were subject to the extraterritorial jurisdiction of their own courts, could buy land and houses in the treaty ports and travel in the interior for business purposes; after the Treaty of Shimonoseki concluded in 1895 they could build factories and manage workshops. These treaty ports and concessions were not ruled by a colonial service with ultimate responsibility in London, Paris, Berlin or Tokyo, but by municipal councils established by foreign residents. Foreign consuls and foreign regiments answerable to foreign ministries did exist in the treaty ports, although they did not control the municipal councils.

Foreign self-government, however, was not always pursued by foreign communities: while some treaty ports developed into formidable trading cities, for instance Shanghai, others such as Yichang or Beihai remained backwaters, whatever foreign privileges may have existed. On the other hand, ports such as Nanning in 1907, Pukou in 1915 and Xuzhou in 1922 were opened unilaterally to international trade by China without gaining much interest from foreign traders.[28] Moreover, by 1914 no less then 10 out of the 29 national concessions had no more than a theoretical existence, while the total was further reduced by five during World War I when German, Russian and Austro-Hungarian concessions were liquidated and again between 1925 and 1931, when Britain and Belgium surrendered five of their concessions, including in Hankou. Extraterritoriality was thus on the decline in the republican era, although globalisation boomed. Even as foreign settlements lost their privileges, their populations continued to grow: Hankou, for instance, harboured a handful of foreigners in the 1890s, but dozens of different nationalities lived in the city after World War II.[29] In other cities, moreover, no concessions or settlements existed, and locals and foreigners lived side by side, as in the case of Nanjing, the capital from 1927 to 1949.

While much has been said about foreign gunboats patrolling the Yangzi, the abuse of extraterritorial rights by foreign criminals and the racist attitudes of foreign communities in general, not to mention the presence of military detachments, diplomatic privileges and legal powers, the contribution of foreign settlements to the integration of republican China with a broader international community remains to be assessed. The foreign establishment, for instance, maintained concessions and settlements in which local taxes and foreign investment led to massive urban infrastructures which rivalled with the very best internationally, ranging from sewage systems, port installations, communication networks, insurance facilities to hospitals, banks and schools. The investment in land, industry and commerce was phenomenal. In the case of France in 1932 this amounted to $200 million, representing about 5 percent of all French foreign investments. While this may seem little, it was proportionally ten times more than the foreign investment from France into China in the early twenty-first century.[30]

Most local people learnt about modern equipment, new technologies, accounting methods and banking systems not via the economic initiatives launched by republican governments, but via the foreign enterprises made possible by concessions and extraterritorial privileges. Foreign communities, however distasteful their presence may have been to nationalist elites, were an effective innovative force in local society: few students could afford to travel all the way to Japan, Europe and the United States to pursue a modern education, but many could acquire knowledge of a myriad of aspects of modern industry and modern governance by living, working, and, increasingly from the 1920s onwards, participating in one of the foreign concessions and settlements. With hindsight, the emergence of hugely complex international concessions in Shanghai and Tianjin within less than a century must have constituted the largest cultural transfer in human history, comparable to the transplantation of entire metropoles from Europe to China, from skyscrapers and departments stores down to pavement slabs and sash windows, and it is unlikely that such transfer could have taken place, at least initially, without the extraterritorial rights allowing business to be conducted outside of the jurisdiction of native authorities — the proof being that most successful local enterprises were established not in native cities but in the foreign concessions, often with foreign partners in order to obtain security of persons and property. To take a concrete example, the transfer of new technologies in the production of soybean processing, as Shannon Brown has demonstrated, was unsuccessful until 1895, not because of any innate incompatibility of modern technology with local conditions, but because a powerful coalition of local merchants and government officials prevented innovation when perceived as a threat. After 1895, when the Treaty of Shimonoseki gave foreigners the legal right to establish factories in the treaty ports, the use of new technology grew rapidly — in both foreign and local firms.[31] As Albert Feuerwerker has noted in his detailed study of the foreign establishment in China, 'While it is not accessible to quantitative measurement, in the long run perhaps the most important (and largely unintended) aspect of foreign manufacturing was its role in the transfer to China of modern industrial technology in the form of machinery, technical skills, and organisation.'[32]

By far the most resented foreign presence was inside the Chinese government itself. As noted above, several government branches, while formally controlled by Beijing and later Nanjing, were largely staffed by foreigners, in particular the Maritime Customs Service, the Post Office and the Salt Administration. The preceding chapter has highlighted how these departments not only substantially enlarged the revenues collected by the central government, but also provided a measure of administrative probity, efficiency and continuity in the republican era. The thesis that these various institutions represented an imperialist control over government finance has long since been denounced as an oversimplification, and it is not the purpose to review these debates here; rather, the point is to show how, despite an increasingly anachronistic situation — eliminated in 1943 — of having extraterritorial staff running large government agencies in an age of national sovereignty, this temporary arrangement, instituted by foreign traders during the Taiping Rebellion in the 1850s to collect taxes which went uncollected by Qing officials, contributed to a cosmopolitan environment in which many local employees were trained in accounting, governance and administration according to high international standards. In short, they contributed to one of the world's most impressive transfers of skills and technologies which turned a millennial empire into a more or less modern state in less than a century.

Robert Hart, the rather autocratic inspector-general who supervised the Maritime Customs from 1863 to 1908, genuinely, if naively, believed that no conflict existed between foreign powers and the national interests of China as he set out to transform the country into a modern state with England providing the models to be followed, even as the entirety of the customs revenue had become pledged to the repayment of foreign loans contracted to pay large indemnities imposed by the Treaty of Shimonoseki in 1895 and after the Boxer Rebellion in 1900.[33] Despite his proclaimed commitment to creating an 'honest and efficient' native administration, no local clerk attained even the grade of assistant during his tenure, although this may have been due to the opposition from higher officials in Beijing to the graduates from mission schools hailing largely from southern provinces, Guangdong in particular. After the founding of the Customs College in 1908, however, recruits were increasingly appointed from a pool of well-trained graduates, leading, for example in 1915 in the Revenue Department, to a proportion of roughly 80 percent of local Indoor Staff among a total of 1525 employees of many nationalities, including British, American, French, Japanese, Dutch, Danish, Portuguese, Norwegian and German. The Outdoor Staff too was largely composed of local employees, although here as well most positions of responsibility were filled by foreigners. On the other hand, the Ministry of Posts and Communications had French nationals as postmaster-generals and foreign staff of about twenty-five, all of them formally subordinated to a local director of the Ministry. The Salt Administration, to take a third and final example, never had more than 40 to 50 foreign employees among a staff in excess of 5,000: they worked mainly as auditors, district inspectors or assistant district inspectors, and were strategically used by conservative officials as pressure points against centrifugal forces.[34]

While the extent of foreign participation thus varied drastically and changed over time from almost complete control in the Maritime Customs to a mere nominal presence in the Salt Administration, it contributed to an unusually international composition in government institutions, facilitated the transfer of administrative skills and added, despite misgivings from nationalist elites, to the shaping of modern state institutions which lasted throughout the republican era — and, some historians have claimed, well beyond 1949. The government itself, moreover, was fully aware of the role of foreigners as conduits of cultural and technological transfer: whether under Yuan Shikai or Chiang Kai-shek, a stream of experts was utilised, from League of Nation technicians, Japanese legal advisers, German army officers, British construction engineers, French postal personnel and

American transportation experts: in the first few years of the republic alone, some of the most prominent advisers included Ariga Nagao, prominent international jurist; George Padoux, expert on public administration; Henry Carter Adams, standardiser of railroad accounts; Henri de Codt, writer on extraterritorial jurisdiction; William Franklin Willoughby, noted political scientist; Frank J. Goodnow, legal adviser; and Banzai Rihachiro, military expert. At less eminent levels, many foreign employees contributed to the country's modernisation, ranging from engineers, clerks, accountants and lawyers to teachers and translators.[35]

Who were the foreigners inhabiting the treaty ports, besides government employees? Just as the literature on 'overseas Chinese' in Southeast Asia has tended to portray sojourners as temporary stayers, and thus marginalises locally born and locally settled communities who became truly cosmopolitan in their understanding of different cultures, so much of the scholarship on 'Westerners' in China has emphasised their transient nature, ignoring how many settled and laid down roots in the country. It is true that many foreign sojourners in China rarely ventured out in the 'native city' and had limited contact with local people, their existence revolving around the expatriate community. However, this idea of 'self-containment' betrays ignorance of the complicated lives led by a diversity of communities in the foreign concessions: many, when as children on their way to school, came across paupers, cripples, beggars, and, on occasions rare but traumatic enough to leave lasting memories, the bodies of babies wrapped in rough cloth to be collected by public health services. Many of the wealthy children were looked after by a local amah, often learning elements of local dialect which parents could not understand and developing long-lasting emotional ties: Jean Bazil, born in Shanghai in 1931, referred all his life to Madeleine, a Christian born in Ningbo, as 'my mother'.[36]

While there is a longstanding tradition among foreign scholars to rightly castigate the so-called 'treaty-port mentality' for its blinkered self-interest, from Arthur Ransome in the 1920s to the more recent work of Robert Bickers,[37] a number of writers have highlighted instead the huge variety of foreign experiences in very different settlements in different parts of the country.[38] Whether British, French, American or Japanese, entire families could be established in the country for generations: in many cases treaty port life was home, regardless of whether or not much contact was established with local people. Many settler families had children, and not all of these were sent to boarding school, as English, American, French, German and Japanese schools in China maintained national curricula — as did also a number of private schools. Many children born of missionary parents or business people grew up in China, some becoming bilingual and profoundly attached to their home country. Robert Tharp and his wife Evangeline were born on opposite sides of China, one in the shadows of the Himalaya, the other on the border of Mongolia. They met at a seaside resort and carried out missionary work in the small town of Lingyuan, where Robert was born and lived for thirty years before arriving on the shores of the United States after World War II without any identity papers: he and his wife were called 'white Chinese', and they would have stayed in China with their children, also born in the country, had it not been for the communist takeover in 1949.[39]

Many foreigners knew and served the country well: as John K. Fairbank himself underlined, 'treaty-port cemeteries are filled with foreigners who understood China well enough to live and die there'.[40] John C. Ferguson (1866–1945) may have been exceptional, but his career certainly illustrates how foreigners could become rooted in China: he came as a missionary in 1887, presided over the beginnings of the University of Nanking, administered Nanyang College, acquired ten Chinese-language newspapers in 1899, served as secretary of the Ministry of Commerce and chief secretary of the Imperial Chinese Railway Administration for a decade after 1902, edited the *Journal of the North China Branch of the Royal Asiatic Society*, helped as vice-president of the Red Cross Society of China, was active in famine relief, became a member of the Chinese delegation to the Washington Conference of 1921, published extensively about Chinese art in both English and Chinese and also found time to amass a vast collection of Chinese art: he left the bulk of it to the University of Nanking.[41]

There were many other examples, including Carl Crow who lived in China for twenty-six years, spoke the language and had deep respect and admiration for the country, conveyed in many of his books, including his *400 Million Customers*.[42] Ida Pruitt, head of hospital social service at the Peking Union Medical College, founded by the China Medical Board of the Rockefeller Foundation in 1917, was born in Penglai, Shandong province, and spoke Chinese from infancy thanks to the care of her amah: she thought of the foreign ways of her missionary parents as rather odd.[43] Pearl Buck too believed that she grew up in a double world, 'the small white clean Presbyterian American world of my parents and the big loving merry not-too-clean Chinese world'; she added that 'there was no communication between them', although her own work, and that of hundreds of others, proved her wrong.[44] As a vast collection of letters, memoirs and biographies show, many foreigners — from Reginald Johnston, tutor of the last emperor, to Innes Jackson, who worked in Wuhan — established lasting friendships, giving the lie to the stereotype of missionaries and traders as invariably narrow and intolerant people.[45]

While some of these long-term residents came from missionary or trading families, refugees also made China their home. The term 'refugee' in the twenty-first century brings to mind migrants from Africa and Asia arriving on the shores of Europe and the United States, but over 100,000 European refugees ended up in republican China, starting with more than 80,000 White Russians after 1917, and continuing with some 20,000 from Germany, Austria, Czechoslovakia, Poland, Lithuania, Estonia and Latvia, the majority impoverished Jews, in the 1930s; some acquired Chinese citizenship.[46] Constantin Rissov, for instance, grew up as a White Russian in Harbin and completely identified with his homeland, acquiring fluency in both language and culture during decades of residence in both republican and communist China — many of them in the gulag.[47]

It was not just foreign residents who often identified sympathetically with China: eminent travellers and writers from all over the world came to stay in the country. While much is known about communist sympathisers such as Agnes Smedley and Edgar

Snow — thanks to unremitting propaganda — it is often overlooked that some of Europe's most brilliant scholars considered China to be the place to be. To take one example, William Empson, one of England's leading literary critics, spent much of his early career at universities in Japan and China after his servant found an unused condom in his room at Magdalene College, Cambridge, and academic doors were closed to him: it is difficult to see a liberal scholar hounded out of a job in England today taking refuge in the People's Republic. And he was not the only original mind to find employment at the National Peking University. In the 1930s Harold Acton worked there, as well as Virginia Woolf's nephew Julian Bell, while W. H. Auden and Christopher Isherwood visited the country.[48]

By far the largest foreign presence, however, were the missionaries, and their many contributions have long been emphasised even by scholars in the PRC.[49] There were well over 8,000 Protestant and several thousand Catholic missionaries in China in 1925, a peak of missionary activity followed by a gradual fall in numbers as foreign journalists joined local nationalists in anti-missionary criticisms and declining home support limited their activities in evangelism, medicine and education. Many of their projects continued to thrive with local support: the thirteen Christian colleges and universities, including three medical schools and two major agricultural colleges, had over 6,000 students in 1934–35, while at the secondary level the missions supported 260 middle schools with an enrollment of 50,000. Among the Christian universities were Hangchow Christian University, Lingnan University, the University of Nanking, St. John's University, Shanghai University, Shantung Christian University, Soochow University and Yenching University: all have recently emerged, again, as leaders in their fields, although their foreign background is often brushed aside.

Higher institutes of learning may have been concentrated in the thriving cities along the coast, but Protestant missionaries, let alone Catholic ones, were present, as early as 1919, in all but a hundred of the 1704 counties in China and Manchuria, many speaking the local dialect and living in close contact with the local population. An example of rural commitment was the Tharp family, mentioned earlier: they provided charity over a period of 30 years in the small town of Lingyuan, including relief to the many refugees from the 1942–43 famine.[50] Many missionaries lived in frontier regions where they were frequently harassed by bandits and communist troops, acquiring in the process a more profound knowledge of rural conditions than the central government in Nanjing: missionaries such as George Shepherd, whose mission post in the remote Shaowu region was destroyed by the communists in 1931, was more acutely aware of the appeal and threat of communism in the countryside than the naive reports compiled by urban journalists, whether local or foreign.[51]

As Albert Feuerwerker notes, one of the reasons why missionary activities increased so much in the decades following the Boxer rebellion is that so many links were forged with domestic forces of reform, whether in educational reform or public health: ''Young China'' of the 1910s and 1920s was frequently the product of missionary schools', whether urban reformers, leading journalists or professional sociologists. Missionaries were often at the forefront of social reform, for instance education for women, encouraged by the founding of Ginling College in Nanjing in 1915, the scientific study of agriculture, represented by the School of Agriculture and Forestry of the University of Nanking, and modern medicine, symbolised by the Faculty of Medicine and the Faculty of Dentistry of the West China Union University in Chengdu. Much has been written about the use of gunboats and foreign troops by self-righteous if not bloodthirsty missionaries to settle the many anti-missionary riots which marked the nineteenth century, but in the period which concerns us here — the first half of the twentieth century — riots were sporadic and force was rarely applied: many missionaries welcomed the overthrow of the Qing and viewed the new republic with its religious freedom as their own.[52]

Beyond missionary involvement, the educational establishment profited from huge contributions made via the mission boards, with the Rockefeller Foundation alone spending US $37 million in China between 1913 and 1933, a sum which was only topped by the US $117 million the foundation spent in the United States.[53] An even more telling example of large-scale international help can be found in famine relief: in the case of the northwest famine of 1920–21, for example, the many foreign residents, foreign charitable enterprises and foreign relief agencies made a significant difference. Not only did the American Red Cross intervene rapidly, but a permanent multinational relief organisation was set up in the autumn of 1921, joining seven societies in a non-political body called the China International Relief Commission with headquarters in Beijing: financed by the Chinese government, public contributions, missionary gifts and foreign aid, the commission built 2,000 miles of new roads in the following fifteen years, also digging 5,000 wells, three large irrigation canals and building a thousand miles of river embankments.[54] Privately operated, missionary influenced, philanthropic enterprises could be dismissed as 'irrelevant', and some readers might well want to emphasise the extent of famine in republican China, but the reality is that, however horrific hunger was for its victims, it never created as much havoc as under the empire, when in 1876–79 alone as many as 13 million people died. A railway system which carried grain to the disaster area in 1920–21, lay experts visiting the region and international relief agencies assisting local and central government efforts limited a famine potentially as disastrous as the 1876–79 precedent to half a million deaths.[55] A similar scenario, but complicated by a full-fledged war, characterised the famine in Henan in 1942–43, one of the worst of the republican era when 2 million people died. After 'liberation', in peacetime, at least 30 million people would perish in 1959–62 alone in a man-made famine of which the world remained ignorant for many years. In those years the Communist Party made sure that the famine was confined to the countryside, ring-fencing the cities and limiting starvation to ordinary farmers, supposedly the backbone of the party. Journalists such as Edgar Snow excitedly wrote about famine in the republican era but had not a word to say about the Great Famine under socialism, since their information was dependent on the communist leadership.[56]

Historians of different persuasions, in and out of China, used to condemn the imperialism of foreigners and their activities in China, but more recent scholarship has not been so unilaterally critical. A more balanced view of the treaty ports, as Frances Wood has argued, might at least allow for some achievements, including the recognition of their role as a conduit of those foreign ideas, methods and institutions — from female education to modern medicine — that played a crucial part in the country's modernisation and have been enthusiastically embraced by its political elites.[57] After all, should we be surprised that the cities which lead the country in the twenty-first century, from Tianjin and Shanghai to Wuhan and Hong Kong, are the ones which had an earlier foreign presence? European empires, formal or informal, were powerful agents of globalisation, contributing to the creation of multicultural societies and intensifying the flows of people, goods, technologies and ideas across borders. But while the foreign establishment may have facilitated the appearance of modern governance, it did not move China into the modern world: as this book has argued so far, and as the next chapter will show in greater detail, this was done by local people of all backgrounds, many of them quick to seize upon the new opportunities afforded by a more open and diverse environment. Highly educated elites in a wide variety of fields, from diplomacy to aviation technology, were not only clued up on international trends but keen to open their country and propel it among the ranks of the developed nations, as we see next.

# 4  Open Minds

As the last chapter has shown, borders in the first half of the twentieth century were open as never before. This openness resulted not only in large flows of people moving in and out of the country, but also in China developing a remarkable degree of international engagement, from regular participation in international conferences to eager contribution to international bodies like the League of Nations. China was not merely a follower, however keen, of foreign trends: for example, several top lawyers, flawlessly bilingual and trained in the very best law schools in Europe, became judges at the International Court of Justice in The Hague. Similar observations can be made about many other fields, ranging from paleo-anthropology to aviation technology, as a constant inflow of knowledge to a country open to new ideas created highly educated professionals who were able to match their foreign peers in many fields.

Not only wealthy elites, but ordinary people too could be conversant with the world beyond China, as knowledge of the foreign was disseminated via text, image and sound (illustrated magazines and radio programmes). A global outlook was also fostered by a modern education system, as even small local schools insisted on dispensing the rudiments of a liberal education: the biographies of great foreign figures like Lincoln, Washington, Napoleon, Watt and Edison were read in cash-stripped county schools deep inside the hinterland. The extent and diversity of religious expression in republican China is often downplayed, although for the first time religious movements persecuted as 'heterodox' under the empire were allowed to exist in a climate of relative tolerance. Christian missionaries or Japanese monks could exercise their activities with an unprecedented degree of freedom (both could preach to prisoners), and local religions remained influential (the religious diversity of the republican period has survived in Taiwan to this day). Culture, finally, bloomed in the absence of a monopoly on power and knowledge. Cinema comes to mind, but other creative fields have been overshadowed, such as photography, including the elegant nudes taken by Chen Chuanlin, Huang Banruo and Chen Bingde, or classical music, for instance the modern compositions which mixed popular folk songs with atonal counterpoint by Chou Wen-chung.

## International China

There is no standard text in English on the diplomatic history of twentieth-century China. As William C. Kirby has argued, the paucity of reliable studies on diplomatic history is all the more regrettable since the accomplishments of the republican era in the field of diplomacy are nothing less than stunning. While it has been common to portray the era as one of political dissolution and social disintegration, one of the major successes of republican diplomacy has yet to be explained: not only did China inherit a vast expanse including Manchuria, Mongolia and Tibet, but it managed successfully to defend and maintain these distant and highly contested borders, often diplomatically, with the result that the national space taken over by the People's Republic in 1949 corresponded to the borders of the Qing empire.

Chapter 2 noted how empire and nation are often conflated in the case of China, for instance when historical claims for 'national unity' based on the borders achieved by the Qing are uncritically accepted, and in the portrayal of the increased encroachments by Japan in Manchuria as an 'imperialist expansion' against which republican China was to weak to respond effectively. Yet, as William C. Kirby has observed, it is somewhat ironic that after the success of the anti-Manchu movement in overthrowing the ruling Qing, successive republican governments should mobilise in defence of the Manchu homeland. After all, while Chinese migrants had begun to settle in Manchuria in the eighteenth century, migration to

Manchuria from China was only legalised in 1907. While China was unable to prevent Japanese control over Manchuria, a globally orchestrated campaign of diplomatic efforts together with an uncompromising attitude of non-recognition resulted in the Japanese-administered region of Manzhouguo being denied any semblance of legality: only El Salvador recognised the new Manchu homeland, and Manchuria was formally returned to Chinese rule by both the United States and the Soviet Union after 1945.[1] A similar account could be given of other regions, including Tibet and Inner Mongolia, as most regions of the imperial realm were under republican control in 1945 — while, as noted in the last chapter, all foreign concessions had been surrendered and extraterritorial rights abolished in 1943 (with the exception of Hong Kong). Both achievements — the removal of internal frontiers and the defence of imperial borders to obtain national sovereignty — depended not only on international goodwill, as foreign powers preferred a united China to a divided one, but also on the efforts of several generations of highly successful diplomats with widespread global connections.

It is not the purpose here to recount the diplomatic history of republican China, but merely to highlight the extent to which the country was an active agent seeking full participation in the international community — despite a very negative appraisal of its achievements in conventional history. Immediately after the defeat of the Sino-Japanese War in 1895 the Qing started participating in international conferences. The empire sent a high-ranking diplomat to the First and Second Peace Conferences held at The Hague in 1899 and 1907, contributing to the first formal statements of the law of war in an emergent body of international law. Most of the Hague Conventions were ratified by China in 1917, thus marking the country's entrance into international conventions and paving the way to a declaration of war on Germany and Austria as called for by its new international obligations: China sent 140,000 labourers to France as a contribution to the war effort.[2] The country's sustained involvement in international alliances culminated a few decades later, as China was internationally recognised, thanks to its performance in diplomacy and war, as a 'great power' during World War II, participating as one of the key partners in a global balance of power and gaining a permanent seat on the Security Council of the new United Nations.

Lu Zhengxiang, one of China's most gifted diplomats and several times Minister of Foreign Affairs, did much to further the diplomatic interests of the country during the Hague conferences, but the diplomatic effort to include China into international conventions, abolish extraterritorial rights and defend the imperial borders were also served extremely well by other cosmopolitan politicians. Alfred Sze, Wellington Koo (Gu Weijun), Wang Chengting and W. W. Yen all belonged to the 'Anglo-American Group' dedicated to the elevation of the country's international status. This extraordinary corps graduated from Ivy League universities, becoming eloquent and effective spokesmen for China, being at home in London, Washington, Geneva or Beijing. Educated at St. John's University, Shanghai, and in international law and diplomacy at Columbia University, Wellington Koo was one of the most influential delegates at the Paris Peace Conference in 1919. He was involved in the formation of the League of Nations and acted as China's first representative to it. Later he was one of the founding members of the United Nations in 1945 and was such a respected diplomat that he was made judge and vice-president in the International Court of Justice at The Hague in 1956.

Most of these diplomats not only managed to maintain the legitimacy of republican China's borders, but were able to survive frequent government changes and provide an impressive degree of success in foreign affairs. During the Washington Conference of 1921–22, for instance, the performance of Alfred Sze and Wellington Koo resulted in the withdrawal of Japan from Shandong and the retrocession of Weihaiwei from Great Britain, in respect for China's sovereignty from the nine powers and in an increase in the customs tariff. Protracted negotiations at this and further international conferences, including the Tariff Revision Conference in 1926, led to the achievement of tariff autonomy in 1928. Chapter 2 argued that there was a significant degree of continuity and independence in many republican institutions: nowhere was this more true than in the

Ministry of Foreign Affairs, in particular in the person of Wellington Koo, who joined the ministry in 1912 as a young man and negotiated, three decades later, the final rendition of all extraterritorial rights from Britain and the United States as Ambassador to the Court of St. James in 1943.[3]

But global links were also forged by others, as China became a participant in almost every major international conference in a whole range of fields, from penal reform to human genetics. In law, for instance, a number of highly respected jurists made lasting contributions to international organisations. Wang Chonghui, already encountered in Chapter 2 and Chapter 3, published in Great Britain the standard English version of the German Civil Code in 1907. He was elected deputy judge of the International Court of Justice in 1921. Wang Chonghui, like the group of diplomats mentioned above, was keen to abolish extraterritoriality and strove to contribute towards this goal by implementing reform as Head of the Judicial Yuan, the highest judicial organ and one of the five branches of government in China. Others pursued equally successful careers in international organisations. Zheng Tianxi (F. T. Cheng), born in 1884, was a sophisticated lawyer who was trained abroad and had extensive experience of international law. The first student from China to receive an LLD in England, Vice-Minister of Justice from 1931–34, Zheng Tianxi had joined the judiciary in 1917 to supervise the translation of law into English. He participated in the Washington Conference in 1921–22 and toured the country with the Commission on Extraterritoriality in 1925: his successful career, like that of others engaged in the legal profession, reflected a desire from his early youth onwards to have extraterritoriality abolished. He was a judge at the International Court of Justice at The Hague from 1936 to 1949.[4]

China closely collaborated with the League of Nations in a number of domains, for instance embracing new regulations for industrial production. As an example, farmers in the silk industry were required to disinfect their buildings, as international standards agreed at the League of Nations were gradually introduced. China also turned to the League of Nations for guidance on standards which were not binding by treaty, for instance in education, where the

'Becker Commission' provided advice on the reorganisation and centralisation of higher education, an objective vigorously pursued by the Nationalist Party.[5] And often China was at the forefront in Asia in signing international conventions promoted by the League of Nations: the International Convention for the Suppression of the Traffic in Women and Children, which China signed in 1922, for instance, had no other signatory from Asia and Africa, except for Thailand (although South Africa and India were represented by the British Empire).[6] China's participation was reflected in the number of registrations of treaties it deposited during the first decade of the League of Nations, namely thirteen, which, while only about a tenth that of most large European countries, was nonetheless the highest of any non-European country except Canada (19) and Japan (21).[7] In the case of drugs policy, which also became part of the League of Nations' purview, China had actually initiated international efforts to curb narcotics, as the International Opium Commission which convened in Shanghai in 1909 and the second Hague Convention (1912–14) grew directly out of the bilateral treaties the Qing had negotiated separately with a number of foreign powers, first with France in 1900, followed by a Commercial Treaty with Britain in 1902 and an opium treaty with Germany in 1903. In addition, the Sino-British Ten Year Agreement of 1907 also outlawed the importation of opium from overseas.[8]

Besides the pursuit of high diplomacy within the international community, central governments and local associations alike ceaselessly pushed for participation in international activities. For instance, China was involved at every level with the international movement for prison reform. As early as 1876, Guo Songtao, the first resident minister in Britain, advised the Qing to send a delegation to the international conference on penal reform in Stockholm, but his proposals were ignored. With the New Policies initiated in the wake of the Boxer Rebellion, however, delegates were sent to almost every major conference on penal administration, from the Eighth International Penitentiary Congress in Washington in 1910 to the International Conference on Penology in Czechoslovakia in 1930 and the Sixth International Conference on the Unification of Penal Law in Copenhagen in the summer of 1935. China was no mere follower of prison reform: from the very first years of the republic the central government was keen to abide by internationally agreed standards of treatment for prisoners of war (POWs), while China was a signatory to the Geneva Declaration on the Treatment of Prisoners of War in July 1929 — which was translated into Chinese and publicly circulated the same month. In August 1934, to take another example, China adopted the minimum standards for the treatment of prisoners set by a penal commission of the League of Nations, which included the principles of separation of different categories of prisoners, the provision of adequate clothing and bedding, minimum standards in food and vocational training, the protection of prisoners' health, and the minimum use of corporal punishment. In an age of illiberal regimes in Italy, Portugal, Spain, Germany, the Soviet Union and Japan, full acceptance of these standards put China firmly among the more progressive countries in penal matters. It might by argued that only a few model prisons were administered according to these penal ideals, but profuse and precise archival evidence shows that by the 1930s these standards were actively pursued at every level of penal administration, including county gaols.[9]

Not all of these international efforts, of course, would be welcomed by historians who have the advantage of hindsight: China's participation in the international eugenics movement, for instance, was also profound, as delegates not only attended international conferences, but experts in fields as diverse as sociology and genetics published a wide range of texts on the subject, ranging from scholarly debates to university textbooks, some of which culminated in legal efforts to enforce a ban on the marriage of people deemed to be 'unfit'.[10] The point of this section, however, is not to judge the intellectual merit of the international movements and conferences which took place between the two World Wars, but to highlight the extent to which China participated in them. The next section looks in more detail at the intellectual links forged at home with the rest of the world by cosmopolitan scholars in virtually every field of knowledge, from avionics to zoology.

## Polyglot Knowledge

In a recent article on the 1930s art scene in Shanghai, Zheng Shengtian recounts how, as a young student browsing through a used bookshop in 1962, he stumbled upon a study on *Arts from around the World in 1935* translated and compiled by Lin Fengmian in 1936. Lin Fengmian (1900–91) himself had become a recluse after being denounced as politically incorrect in the early 1950s, his name was rarely mentioned and his work was banned. The small volume was part of a series entitled *The World in 1935* and introduced the reader to the many artistic activities in Europe during that year, including Fauvism, Cubism, a retrospective of the German painter Max Liebermann and a review of exhibitions held in Paris and Brussels. As the book series shows, Shanghai, in the 1930s, was fully involved in the global art scene, with artists promoting modern styles such as Surrealism and Fauvism, many having studied abroad and organised their own art societies.[11]

Lin Fengmian, who had studied in France in 1919, was then at the height of his creative powers as founding president of the Hangzhou Academy of Art, organising major art exhibitions in Shanghai and Nanjing while publishing and painting in a climate of academic innovation and artistic freedom. In his article, Zheng Shengtian reveals how Lin was arrested in 1968 and locked up at the Number Two Detention Centre in Shanghai, but does not say that the body of his work was largely destroyed during the Cultural Revolution. Lin finally managed to move to Hong Kong in 1977, and died in 1991. His paintings had been accepted by major collections in Europe as early as 1922 and his work can be found today in leading museums in Hong Kong, Taiwan and the United States, including the Guggenheim Museum. As the People's Republic gradually emerges from decades of ignorance about its own past, what is notable in Zheng's article is not only the author's sense of amazement at what was accomplished before 1949, but also the narrow focus on one particular scholar. Lin Fengmian, gifted as he may have been, was hardly a lonely genius: there were literally tens of thousands of creative individuals who were at the top of their fields, fully clued up with the rest of the world in the decades before the communist takeover.

A mere perusal of the *Catalogue of Books Published in the Republican Era* gives an idea of what was accomplished: in twenty volumes well over 100,000 books are briefly presented in all fields of knowledge, from literature, art, law, philosophy, religion, politics and medicine to science.[12] Whatever the discipline covered, it would be difficult to find many publications that did not adopt a global frame of reference, often explicitly, as in the case of many translations, compilations or general introductions such as Lin Fengmian's overview of art in 1935. The catalogue seems impressive and is certainly useful as a research tool for the republican period, but, as historians in touch with primary sources know, it is far from complete, as it is based on the collections of three libraries only (Beijing, Shanghai and Chongqing). And it does not include the many books which must have disappeared between 1949 and 1986, when the first volume of the catalogue came out. In the volume on law, containing some 4400 titles, a mere twenty-five books on penology are listed: for every one of these titles the dedicated sleuth can find another one in a library elsewhere, the catalogue being particularly incomplete for the first decade of the Republic.[13] Neither does the catalogue include books published in one of the other 16 languages commonly used in newspapers and periodicals, nor, for that matter, does it mention these periodicals themselves, of which there were well over 20,000 according to an inventory published in 1961 that explicitly excludes politically 'unworthy' material, from 'reactionary material' to 'religious affairs'.[14] Not recorded either in the catalogue are the many books and periodicals published abroad but bought, read and circulated in the republican era: in 1931 China was the sixth largest subscriber outside the United States of the *Astrophysical Journal,* hardly a page turner.[15] The amount of published material, in short, constitutes a strong testimony of the considerable achievements of the republican era. Foreign material, either in the original or in translation, was widely available before 1949.

Quantity matters, but so does quality: of the dozens of books on penology — to expand on the example given above — some were general introductions, compiled by the lawyers, judges, magistrates, prison officers, procurators and sociologists who participated in international conferences and introduced important innovations from abroad in talks, lectures, articles and books. Others, however, were original studies which contributed to the circulation of global knowledge. Yan Jingyue, for instance, produced a doctoral dissertation at the University of Chicago based on case studies of prisoners interviewed in Beijing Number One Prison. He also published articles in English in the *Howard Journal*, sponsored by the international Howard League for Penal Reform.[16] Most of the crucial contributions, however, appeared not in the form of books but in the dedicated periodicals which instantly conveyed to an expert audience the latest developments in penological knowledge: besides the prestigious *China Law Review* (*Faxue jikan*, continued as *Faxue zazhi* in 1931) published in Shanghai from 1922 to 1940, as well as the government-sponsored *Official Journal on Judicial Administration* (*Sifa gongbao*), published from 1912 to 1938, at least six, but possible twice as many, journals specifically dedicated to prison reform circulated among prison staff.[17]

In the field of sociology, to take another example, the catalogue records some 2,600 publications, yet here again quality mattered as much as quantity. Maurice Freedman, Professor of Social Anthropology at the University of Oxford as well as a distinguished sinologist who had spent two years in China in 1949–50, believed that outside Europe and the United States, 'China was the seat of the most flourishing sociology in the world, at least with respect of its intellectual quality'.[18] Indeed, the Chinese Sociological Society, at its first national convention held in Shanghai in 1930, attracted 200 delegates. Doctoral dissertations in sociology were obtained abroad as early as 1912, when Y. Y. Tsu completed his study on 'The Development of Chinese Philanthropy' at Columbia University, while some of the foreign-trained sociologists went on to write scholarly monographs in English, French, German or Japanese. A dozen independent sociology departments existed by the 1930s, while in 1927 some sixty universities in China offered over 300 courses in sociology, taught by local and foreign staff who often collaborated in path-breaking studies:[19] Sidney Gamble's *Peking: A Social Survey* is one example of a classic still referred to today, John L. Buck's comprehensive *Land Utilization in China*, mentioned in Chapter 2, yet another.

Foreigners may have collaborated with locals in China, but the flow went both ways: to this day sociologists interested in drug usage refer to the pioneering work of Bingham Dai, *Opium Addiction in Chicago*, originally published in 1937 and reprinted in 1970, few realising that the author was Chinese. Dai Bingyeung (1899–1996) graduated from St. John's University in Shanghai, studied under Edward Sapir at Yale and received a doctorate in sociology in Chicago under Harry Stack Sullivan: he was the first sociologist to study the consumers of drugs rather than the policies on drugs, breaking a taboo by proclaiming value in the ethnographical study of illicit behaviour and interviewing opium and heroin users in Chicago's inner city.[20] Such was the growth of sociology and the volume of its intercultural traffic that by the 1930s some of the larger departments compared favourably with sociology departments of similar size in Europe and the United States.

That many similar observations could be made about other fields should hardly surprise us, since Chinese students outnumbered any other foreign nationality at American universities by 1930: knowledge in all areas was hotly pursued.[21] Rough estimates indicate that some 40,000 students acquired degrees abroad and returned to become political and intellectual leaders in China before 1949, about half from the United States, a quarter from Japan and another quarter from Europe: republican China, as C. P. Fitzgerald noted, was led by men of double culture, 'and no understanding of China which ignores this fact is possible'.[22] Many students not only acquired academic degrees, but also lasting links which turned out to be very useful throughout their careers, in particular after 1949. Yuen Ren Chao (Zhao Yuanren, 1892–1982), born in Tianjin in 1892, is one example among many: a true polyglot, he not only became a famed linguist, acquiring fluency in several European languages and many local dialects in China, but studied mathematics at Cornell University and obtained a doctorate in philosophy from Harvard University. The point is not only to stress his contributions to the field of Chinese language studies, for instance his standard *Grammar of Spoken Chinese*, but also to note that he was recognised as a leader in the more general field of linguistics: in 1945, for instance, he served as president of the Linguistic Society of America. When the communists seized the mainland, he decided to stay in the United States.

Even more telling is the contribution of physicists trained in Germany and the United States.[23] Tsung-Dao Lee (Li Zhengdao, born in 1926) was educated in Shanghai, Hangzhou and Kunming, leaving China only after World War II on a Chinese Government Scholarship to complete a doctoral dissertation at the University of Chicago in 1946: he worked on high energy particle physics and obtained the Nobel Prize in 1957 jointly with Chen Ning Yang (Yang Zhenning), who also attended university in Kunming before moving to the University of Chicago with a scholarship in 1946: their educational background in the republican era prepared them well for groundbreaking research. And they were not alone. Chien-Shiung Wu (Wu Jianxiong, 1912–97), who attended Suzhou Women's Normal School before being admitted at the University of Nanking in 1929, also studied in the United States for a doctorate in physics and became the first female instructor in the Physics Department of Princeton University. Her contribution to the field was such that some felt that she should have shared the Nobel Prize in 1957 with Chen Ning Yang and Tsung-Dao Lee, whom she assisted in the development of parity laws. She later became the first female president of the American Physical Society in 1975. As much as the mainland was enriched immeasurably by the global connections patiently established by tens of thousands of scholars over several decades, it was Hong Kong, Taiwan and the United States which profited most from the communist closure of the country in 1949, keeping or attracting some of the world's brightest minds.

Most of these examples have focused on the top level of research in the humanities and the sciences, but many of the 100,000 books mentioned above were designed as simple introductory texts for popular audiences. Periodicals specifically designed to impart global information to rural readers used simplified language: the *Christian*

*Farmer*, for instance, was read by tens of thousands, its success dependent on the way in which information from all over the world was presented to rural communities.[24] Yet the most significant vector of global knowledge was probably school: 'It was in the high school in N. that I heard for the first time about service to the community and not to the family only, although the teachers also stressed the importance of filial piety. We were told about the duties of a citizen, about patriotism, and the sacrifices we must make to make China strong. We were taught how to behave at public meetings, how to get along with people, how to keep public parks and premises clean. We learned Western history and got acquainted with the different constitutions. We read the biographies of great Western figures: Lincoln, Washington, Napoleon, Watt, Edison. English fiction acquainted us with Western love, so different from the Chinese. At school I got my first notion of natural science and Western philosophy. At school I heard Western music for the first time', as a young man who grew up in a village in north China reminisced.[25]

This is not the place to discuss the extent of schooling in republican China, except to note that conservative estimates may have to be revised as archival sources finally become accessible to professional historians and confirm some of the positive comments made by contemporaries. One traveller noted as early as 1920 how even in a small up-river town in Zhejiang province, the two government schools had blackboards, modern maps and new charts, while pupils were dressed in uniform and instruction was provided in most subjects from English to singing.[26] Only a few years after the fall of the empire, Lowes Dickinson, who ridiculed the notion of an unchanging China and appreciated the fast pace of change under the republic, noticed a school in a tiny village a thousand miles from the coast: the walls were hung with drawings of birds and beasts, of the human skeleton and organs, while there were also maps of China and of the world. The children even produced an English reading-book: as Dickinson sympathetically noted, their linguistic abilities may not have amounted to much, but they could say 'cat' when shown a picture of the animal, which was more than he could do in Chinese.[27] In the north of China, as Sidney Gamble, the sociologist mentioned above, observed, a majority of villages established modern schools in the decades following the Boxer Rebellion, and the percentage of families that had children in school ranged from 10 to 25 percent.[28] The situation was similar in many villages in the south, where village leaders and rich families promoted modern schools, despite insufficient school equipment and lack of centralisation in these local efforts.[29] As Elizabeth VanderVen has recently shown on the strength of archival material, even a single county in north China could have hundreds of modern primary schools, as rural communities pursued a variety of strategies to raise funds for education in their enthusiastic quest for modernity.[30]

It is true that not all aspects of the country's discovery of the world were equally laudable, as schoolbooks projected a hierarchical vision of humanity in which unequally endowed 'races' were seen to compete for survival. The opening sentence of a chapter on 'human races' in a 1920 textbook for middle schools, for instance, declared that 'among the world's races, there are strong and weak constitutions, there are black and white skins, there is hard and soft hair, there are superior and inferior cultures. A rapid overview shows that they are not of the same level.' Even in primary schools, readings on racial politics became part of a curriculum with a strong nationalist content: 'Mankind is divided into five races. The yellow and white races are relatively strong and intelligent. Because the other races are feeble and stupid, they are being exterminated by the white race. Only the yellow race competes with the white race . . . China is the yellow race.'[31] But even if many people who benefited from a modern education came to identify themselves and others in terms of 'race' during the republican period, their knowledge of and interest in the world by far surpassed anything hitherto achieved. And the illiterate too were immersed in global images and global sounds, as movies, radio and exhibitions regularly punctuated social life in the republican era — as we see briefly at the end of this chapter.

# Religious Diversity

Any visitor to Shanghai today can see relics of a more open age in some of the churches, temples, mosques and synagogues which have somehow survived destruction under communism: the Orthodox Eastern Church with its five domes in peacock blue, the Xujiahui Cathedral, known as St. Ignatius Cathedral, a brick-red Gothic structure built in 1906 by Jesuits as the largest at the time in all of East Asia, the Small Peach Garden Mosque, the city's most important mosque dating from 1917, the Ohel Moishe Synagogue, begun by refugees in 1907 and moved twenty years later to Ward Road, the ivy-covered Tudor-style Community Church constructed in 1924 as a non-denominational church for Protestants, or the Jade Buddha Temple, erected in 1882 and lavishly reconstructed in 1918–28 to house jade statues brought from Burma by an overseas Chinese, are but a few of the many religious sites which were scattered all over Shanghai before 1949. And religious activity was not restricted to a few treaty ports, as freedom of press, freedom of association and freedom of religion enabled many faiths to thrive during the republican era.

As we have seen in Chapter 3, the missionary presence reached a peak in the 1920s, as Protestants and Catholics made full use of the religious freedom declared by the Republic of China and took a leading role in social reform, opening schools, colleges, hospitals, orphanages and refuges. One of the results of greater religious freedom was a much higher visibility of successful conversions, no longer drawn exclusively from the lower classes as was the case before the 1880s. Lu Zhengxiang (mentioned above), several times Minister of Foreign Affairs, was a Catholic who retired to and died in a Benedictine monastery in Bruges; C. T. Wang (Wang Zhengting), also Minister of Foreign Affairs, was a Christian, as was W. W. Yen (Yan Huiqing), a veteran diplomat and son of a pastor. Sun Yatsen himself was baptised in Macau, while his widow was the daughter of a Methodist Episcopal pastor from North Carolina; Chiang Kai-shek converted in 1931 and demonstrated his goodwill by promising to protect clergymen, pastors and mission property in 1926, despite mounting anti-Christian sentiment. Other converts included the general Feng Yuxiang, received by the Methodist Episcopal Church in 1911: he became a 'Christian General' who persuaded or else commanded many of his men to receive Holy Communion and participate in mass conversions.

Major converts were in charge of prestigious establishments of higher education such as Tsinghua University in Beijing (Mei Yiqi), Fudan University in Shanghai (Ma Liang) and Nankai University in Tianjin (Zhang Boling).[32] Not only was the General Secretary of China's YMCA a local Christian (C. T. Wang, elected in 1915), but by 1920, some thirty percent of YMCA members in China were local citizens.[33] By 1932 it was reported that some 400,000 Roman Catholics were in ecclesiastical districts headed by local priests. While Christianity initially came to China, the flow also reversed, albeit slowly, reinforcing the many threads which integrated republican China with the rest of the world: in 1926, for instance, six local priests were raised to the episcopacy, journeyed to Rome and were consecrated by the Pope in St. Peter's, while on the Protestant side local converts represented China at the Madras meeting of the International Missionary Council in 1938 and established close contacts with Indian Christianity a few years later.[34]

Not everybody welcomed religious freedom in the republican era: a politically diverse climate also resulted in anti-Christian movements and a widespread view among intellectuals that religion in general was an obstacle to progress. This did not prevent many converts from contributing to a thriving publishing culture, which easily surpassed, in quantity and quality, what had been produced in the nineteenth century: freedom of the press led to more than 115 Roman Catholic periodicals in 1937, of which more than half were wholly or partly in Chinese.[35] One of the most striking developments of the republican period, however, was the emergence of an autonomous theology and independent churches. The Church Self-Government Society had 330 branches by 1924, a mere eighteen years after its foundation in Shanghai in 1906. The Church of Christ in China, formed in 1927, had links to numerous representatives of both foreign and local churches. Its local leader was Zheng Qingyi, who was one of the few non-European delegates to the World Missionary

Conference in Edinburgh (1910) when he was only thirty. He became an extensive traveller with global connections.[36]

While most of these examples come from the cities, even in the countryside the presence of Chinese Christians increased over time,[37] occasionally independently from the main congregations: churches such as the Jesus Family and Wang Mingdao's Christian cult captured a growing proportion of the religious population.[38] These independent churches often led to syncretic movements which demonstrated the vigour with which 'foreign' religion was popularly appropriated and indigenised. This was the case for the True Jesus Church (*Zhen Yesujiao*), founded by Barnabas Dong in Beijing in 1917, a movement which owed its origins to the Pentecostal revival among the Chinese Christians of Los Angeles around 1906,[39] as well as of the Little Flock (*Xiao qun*) founded in Fuzhou around 1928 by Ni Tuosheng (*alias* 'Watchman Nee').[40] Both were major denominations by 1949, although the actual numbers of converts are difficult to estimate; the figures of 1 million Protestants and 3 million Catholics were given by the communist regime after their takeover of the mainland.[41]

The Russian Orthodox Church also thrived strikingly, mainly as a consequence of the revolution in Russia and a large influx of refugees. Far more significant, however, was the revival of Buddhism. Yang Wenhui (1837–1911), called the 'Father of the Modern Buddhist Renaissance', established a publishing house for Buddhist texts in Nanjing in the 1860s, travelled to England and France in 1878, imported several hundred sutras and sutra commentaries from Japan, sent surviving texts from China to Nanjo Bunyu, a leading Buddhist in Japan, and collaborated with the missionary Timothy Richard on a translation of the *Treatise on Awakening the Faith in the Great Vehicle* in English in 1894 (it was eventually published in 1907).[42] Others followed, for instance Taixu (1890–1947), who was exposed not only to the writings of influential reformers such as Kang Youwei and Liang Qichao, but also to foreign philosophers such as Bakunin, Proudhon and Marx, and attempted to make Buddhism more compatible with modern trends of thought. Taixu toured Europe, the United States and Japan for nearly nine months in 1928–29, encountering scholars of Buddhism as well as proponents of Christianity. He helped set up chapters of a World Buddhist Institute in Paris, and on his return promoted the Library of the World Buddhist Institute at Wuchang as a centre for the collection of Buddhist literature in different languages, trying to close the gap between foreign and local scholarship. Later, during World War II, he organised Buddhist delegations to Burma, India, Singapore, Malay and Vietnam; some of his disciples moved to Taiwan after 1949, from where centres of Chinese Buddhism were established worldwide.[43] Taixu was part of a trend: dozens of periodicals appeared in the republican era, many directly engaging with global issues related to science, medicine, philosophy and theology, presenting themselves as the modern face of Buddhism.

Buddhism was reinforced rather than weakened by its inclusion in a modern world, as millions were both 'Buddhist' and 'modern'.[44] Holmes Welch may have expressed doubts about the actual vigour of Buddhism in his study entitled *The Buddhist Revival in China*,[45] but other contemporary observers were quite impressed by the expansion of religious activities, both during the 1920s and 1930s and after World War II. Over a quarter of a million Buddhist temples still dotted the landscape after the disaster of a protracted world war from 1937 to 1945, and even if many were in a state of disrepair, some having been put to military uses in wartime, the extent of worship was easy to underestimate because so many devotees worshipped at their own household shrines.[46] Foreign travellers frequently mentioned Buddhist building activity in republican China, although, as Welch has underlined, much of this may have been mere replacement of what had been destroyed in the Taiping Rebellion.[47] Whether or not there was more religious activity than during the nineteenth century may be open to debate, but there is little doubt that the 'stirrings of new life under the impact of new conditions' in Buddhism were such that few observers thought, on the eve of the communist takeover, that it would quickly become an insignificant factor in 'new China': the Buddhist religion, in short, used newly acquired freedoms of press and association to project its activities further inland and abroad, adjusting to a new world in a way which made it as vibrant as ever.

Islam also underwent radical changes during the republican era. Derk Bodde has noted that while the many millions of Muslims in China had produced relatively little scholarship during the Qing, as only Arabic could be used as liturgical language, the first published translations of the Koran appeared in the 1920s, while more generally the 1911 revolution marked the beginning of a lively press, 100 Chinese-language Islamic periodicals having been published at one time or another during the republican era. The circulation numbers, however, tended to be rather small, and most were published in Beijing, Shanghai and Nanjing,[48] but followers of the faith were also reached by radio and cinema. Muslim associations were established, and even if many were ephemeral, they contributed to a climate of decreased religious violence involving Islam, despite a number of outbreaks in Xinjiang. This was in stark contrast to the many millions of deaths in rebellions which shook the empire to its foundations in the nineteenth century, whether in Yunnan in 1818–19, 1826–28, 1834–40 and 1853–73 or in the Northwest in 1862–76. The China Muslim Mutual Progress Association (Zhongguo huijiao jujinhui), established in Beijing in 1912 by Wang Haoran, who had returned to Beijing from extensive religious studies in a number of Islamic countries, was the most significant organisation, with branches in provincial capitals and a membership by 1923 of some 3,000. A Chinese Muslim Federation appeared in 1938, mainly to oppose Japanese efforts to rally Muslims against the Nationalist Party.

Wang Haoran was not alone in studying in the Middle East. While much has been written about students seeking wisdom in Europe, the United States and Japan, other destinations too were pursued in a climate of religious freedom: prior to the 1920s, for instance, only a handful ever made the pilgrimage to Mecca every year, but in the following decade well over 800 pilgrims performed the Hajj, despite the relatively high cost ($1,000) of a round trip to Mecca. In 1937, just before the outbreak of war, the numbers had soared to such an extent that 170 pilgrims were on one steamer that set sail for Mecca from Shanghai (in comparison, the largest group in the first three decades of the People's Republic was 19 in 1979, numbers only increasing to over 6,000 a year in 1993).[49] A mere four students went to Muslim countries to study in the 1920s, but here too numbers increased rapidly in the 1930s, as by 1935 eighteen Chinese Muslims were studying in Cairo; they were granted annual fellowships by the Ministry of Education. They translated into Arabic a number of literary texts, not only Tang poetry and the Confucian *Analects*, but also Lin Yutang's *My Country and My People*, while back home they were also behind broadcasts in Arabic over the government radio. Official missions to various parts of the Islamic world — as part of the diplomatic openness noted above — were also dispatched after 1938, while a series of consulates and embassies in Islamic were opened in the 1940s.[50]

With religious freedom also came increased contacts between religions. Protestant missionaries, for instance, viewed Muslims as potential converts. Marshall Broomhall's research on Muslims in China was commissioned by the World Missionary Congress in Edinburgh and published in 1910 as *Islam in China: A Neglected Problem*; and a number of missionaries dedicated their lives to work among Muslims, for instance Mark Botham, F. W. Martin Taylor, W. A. Saunders and Leonard A. Street.[51] While these missionaries may have underestimated the resilience of Islam, a genuine interfaith dialogue did appear between Buddhism and Christianity, the highlight of which was the Buddhist monk Taixu's call, during a speech at West China Union University, for the propagation of Christianity in China and Buddhism in Europe.[52]

Emulation between different faiths also reinvigorated religious practices, the best example being sermons to prisoners. In Beijing Number One Prison the Methodist Church lectured every Monday, the American Board on Friday, the Presbyterian Church on Saturday and the Anglican Church on Tuesday, while Buddhist monks trained in Japan were also busy instilling repentance into prisoners. Chinese Buddhists observed how Christians spread the gospel by visiting prisons and also set up programmes to propagate the faith among convicts in the early 1920s:[53] some prisons even acquired shrines with the image of Bodhidharma, recited mantras with chimes, wooden fish and flutes and followed the dietary restrictions of Buddhism, High

Courts in turn expressing their appreciation to temples who made contributions to local prisons by giving them votive tablets.[54]

Buddhists were also spurred on by Christians in pursuing charitable enterprises, including the establishment of hospitals, orphanages and schools. Interfaith cooperation was perhaps best illustrated by the creation of an Association of Chinese Religious Believers in 1943 by Buddhist, Protestant, Catholic and Muslim representatives 'to advance freedom of religion with special emphasis on spiritual enrichment and social service'.[55] Also noteworthy was the appearance of syncretic religions, some combining Confucianism, Daoism and Buddhism, others adding Islam and Christianity: some of these would have a lecture on the scriptures by a Norwegian Christian and a dancing ceremony by Daoist priests on the same day. While most of these were admittedly confined to privileged elites in the large cities, others were quite popular, for instance the Church of the Five Religions (Wujiao daoyuan), founded in Shandong province in 1921, purporting to harmonise Daoism, Confucianism, Buddhism, Islam and Christianity, and spreading rapidly enough to report seventy-five societies with a membership mounting into the tens of thousands a mere two years later.[56]

## The Arts

Even those who uphold a rather bleak view of the republican era generally accept that culture flourished during the so-called 'New Culture Movement', as intellectuals concerned about the fate of the nation turned to a vernacular style of writing to attack local institutions, establish new periodicals, introduce a whole range of foreign ideas and generally promote cultural renewal. The 'May Fourth Movement', as the movement is also known from the date of a mass demonstration in Beijing against the award of the German leasehold of Jiaozhou to Japan in 1919, has become the founding myth of Chinese intellectuals, generating an enormous amount of literature which has tended to overshadow other popular trends in culture and the arts. However, the 'literary canon' of the May Fourth

Movement is now being questioned, in China and abroad, as scholars move away from the study of established figures such as Mao Dun or Lu Xun, rediscovering instead alternative writers who have been marginalised for decades after 1949. Eileen Chang, for instance, born in Shanghai in 1920, educated in Hong Kong and resident in the United States for the rest of her life after 1955, wrote before 1949 with flair, style and warmth about the cosmopolitan worlds of Shanghai and Hong Kong. Acclaimed as 'the Garbo of Chinese letters' and 'the most talented woman writer in twentieth-century China', her legendary collection of essays and autobiographical reflections, *Written on Water*, was published in 1945.[57]

However, there remains a strong bias in favour of the written word in these alternative histories. In the absence of a monopoly on power and knowledge, many forms of expression besides literature not only flourished, but, in the cosmopolitan climate of the 1930s, attracted reciprocal interest from artists abroad. Republican artists were fascinated with Europe and the United States, and an extraordinary openness to China also marked filmmakers such as Eisenstein and artists such as Mark Tobey. Some well-placed curators, critics and museum directors were very interested in China, refuting simplistic assumptions about a 'one-sided' exchange.[58] The general public in Europe, between 1931 and 1937, was keen too: to take but one example, at least seventeen exhibitions of modern Chinese painting took place in fourteen cities in Europe between 1933 and 1935, a major one in the New Burlington Galleries in London exhibiting 230 works: these exhibitions were widely attended and repeatedly reported in both China and Europe, from brief notices in the *Illustrated London News* to longer appraisals in the *Times*.[59] Self-confidence generated by a climate of mutual respect nurtured the cultural flows between China and Europe. Ideas and techniques were appropriated in a creative search for experimentation, as we will see briefly with respect to cinema, music and photography.

Before 1949, Shanghai's film industry was second only to Hollywood, although the history of cinema in China used to focus on 'left-wing' cinema, leaving out the much more popular genres of the 1920s and 1930s, from cosmopolitan engagement with modernist forms of cinema to unabashedly local inventions such as martial arts movies. Recent work shows how many of the modernist film producers, for instance, admired Hollywood, happily mixing pulp fiction, swashbuckling beauties, physical comedy and the musical with avant-garde techniques to create a celluloid language which appealed to local audiences, as befitted an era that was in dialogue with international trends. Sun Yu, educated in the United States, borrowed liberally from European and American cinemas, as movie star Li Lili's performance in his *Daybreak* (1933) deliberately resonated with that of Marlene Dietrich in Josef von Sternberg's *Dishonoured* (1931). He also used local aesthetic motifs and artistic repertoires to create a style that was both visually stunning and highly appealing to a popular audience, calling it a 'chop-suey' style.[60] Classical costume, knight errant, martial arts and magic spirit movies attracted even larger audiences, capturing not only millions in China, but many more abroad, as the biggest market was in Southeast Asia: the best-sellers were movies such as *The Cave of the Spider Spirit* and *The Swordswoman of Huangjiang*.[61] Exactly how popular were these movies? We know from one line in Zhang Zhen's overview of these vernacular genres that some fifty studios produced about 240 martial arts and magic spirit movies in Shanghai between 1928 and 1932, representing about 60 percent of the total film output.[62] The movies themselves, as is the case with photography and music, remain rare: of the more than 500 movies made in the 1920s, no more than a handful are extant today, thanks to decades of neglect after 1949.

Hong Kong too played a prominent role in the flourishing of the arts from 1893 to 1949, and cinema was no different. In fact, some of the most successful film companies in Shanghai, for instance Lianhua, had their roots in Hong Kong and were founded by filmmakers from Hong Kong, while Hong Kong cinema was much quicker to make the transition to spoken movies than Shanghai. Using Cantonese rather than Mandarin, the Hong Kong film industry served not only Guangdong, Hong Kong and Macau, but also overseas communities in Southeast Asia and North America. By 1935–37, about thirty talkies were produced a year, local studios having a cosmopolitan background which gave them a special edge: the

Daguan Studio, one of the most important, was founded by Moon Kwan Man-ching (Guan Wenqing) and Joe Chiu Shu-sum (Zhao Shushen), both raised and educated in the United States and using capital from California. Hong Kong cinema blossomed even further between 1937 and 1941, thanks to British neutrality and a massive influx of refugees from the mainland, as forty film companies employing 2,000 people produced an average of a hundred movies a year destined to international audiences:[63] little wonder that colonial Hong Kong, after 1949, was able to continue to excel internationally in cinema for many decades in the face of Hollywood expansion, building a global reputation out of all proportion for such a small enclave with producers and actors such as Jackie Chan, Bruce Lee, Tsui Hark, John Woo and Wong Kar-wai.

Photography has also become a topic of interest in recent scholarship. Photographic images have become one of the most important means of communication in the twentieth century, yet we still know more about the history of photography in Bamako, Mali, than about the history of photography in China. The name of Seydou Keita, one of Bamako's portrait photographers, is well known among readers interested in photography outside Europe, but most general historians of visual culture would be hard pressed to recognise the name of Lang Jingshan, China's pre-eminent photographer whose work was exhibited and collected around the globe before the communist takeover. Such was his reputation that among a string of international prizes and nominations he was made a Fellow of the Royal Photographic Association in Britain — unlike Seydou Keita.

As a recent doctoral dissertation shows, Lang Jingshan, like other local art photographers whose work was keenly sought in and out of republican China, transformed the camera by incorporating it with more traditional media, for instance painting.[64] Sophisticated techniques and inventive procedures further led to distinct local styles of visual culture: photos were often painstakingly tinted by hand, while a number of artists even applied oil colours to efface the boundary between 'photography' and 'painting'. The use of calligraphy was unique to photographic practice in China: in a country where mastery of the written language was a sign of social distinction, the educated would often add a verse onto a carte-de-visite, while artists adorned sepia-toned photos of landscapes with entire poems and added a red chop and signature. Collage, composite printing or deliberate blurring during development further complicated the boundary between traditional landscape painting and landscape photography. Lang Jingshan went further than most in composing collage photographs in which many of the 'traditional' signifiers in painting, for instance herons, rockery, rivers, cloudy peaks and even the lonely sage with his walking stick, were brought together in one image, accentuating each photograph with calligraphy in the manner of a traditional painting.

The existence of an open society allowed controversial styles to be explored, for instance nude photography. As a result of historical amnesia, the appearance of nude photography in the 1990s has been hailed as a welcome breach of an entrenched taboo, a show in Guangdong in 2001 being described by a communist news agency as 'the country's first nude photo show'.[65] These commentators are all but oblivious to the fact that photographers such as Pan Dawei, Chen Bingde, Chen Chuanlin, Li Song, Lang Jingshan and others regularly and openly experimented with nude models, the results being exhibited in shows and published in a variety of illustrated magazines before 1949. Photos of nudes by international artists such as Bruno Schulz, Willy Zielke, Bertram Park, George Platt Lynes and Heinz Hajek-Halke circulated publicly during this period, and nude photos by Heinz von Perckhammer, encountering international success, were taken with local models in China and exhibited and reprinted in China.[66]

Lang Jingshan may have obtained world fame before his erasure from the record in the People's Republic for decades after 1949, but he was hardly the country's only photographer, as an abundance of source material shows.[67] Photographic images permeated everyday life, from the pictorial newspaper to the family portrait on the wall. The existence of studio photographers in every town and city is never noted in the field of social history: in contrast to Africa, where dedicated scholars from Europe and Africa have collaborated to reconstruct not only the histories, but also the collections of representative studios,[68] we still know very little about studio photography in China — despite the simple fact that by the 1930s virtually everybody who could save a dollar had made the visit to one of the hundreds of studios kept busy by an incessant demand for portraits. Besides ordinary people, famous actresses and movie stars started using the cartes-de-visite which were already popular in Europe. Not only did they liberally circulate images of themselves among family and friends, but they frequently appeared in illustrated magazines which catered to an audience interested in the lives of the wealthy: screen actresses, society ladies, political leaders, famous artists, wealthy industrialists covered the pages of pictorials like the *Young Companion* (*Liangyou huabao*) or the *Peiyang Pictorial News* (*Beiyang huabao*), their portraits captured by professional photographers and sent to the editor with a signature on the front or back. The same magazines reproduced photographs of places, people and events from around the world, contributing to a sophisticated culture which integrated republican China into a global framework of visual references.

Popular music, too, burgeoned in republican China: international concessions, after all, promoted international types of music, from classical to jazz and chanson. The municipality of the concession in Shanghai paid a subvention to a symphony orchestra consisting of artists of all nations and directed by the Italian Mario Paci, who had been in China for eighteen years by 1935. The orchestra, based as it was in Shanghai, did not trail behind its competitors in Europe and the United States, but instead, as so many other ventures in the republican era, blazed ahead, as Mario Paci played the latest work of contemporary composers, including the compositions of Respighi, de Falla, Ravel, Kodály, Bartók and Hindemith, sometimes in advance of his colleagues elsewhere, and transmitted by radio to a much larger audience. Noted performers, from international prodigy Sergei Rachmaninoff to famous violinist Fritz Kreisler, came to play in China, while a touch of music was imparted en masse in the many movies regularly visited by local audiences. In the capital Nanjing, far away from any concession, a state-of-the-art auditorium was built with ultra-modern equipment, able to hold over 3,000 listeners, and judged by Zhao Meiba, a globally noted baritone trained at the Conservatoire Royale de Bruxelles, to be 'better than many of the well-known ones in other parts of the world'.[69]

Shanghai had a conservatory of music, established in 1927 by Xiao Youmei, a graduate from Leipzig and composer of ballets, chamber music, songs and piano pieces. With C. T. Yan, a graduate of the Geneva Conservatory, he also founded a music department at the Academy of Fine Arts in Beijing in 1921, which had an international staff, while the music department of the Yenching University regularly performed Handel's *Messiah* and Brahms' *Deutches Requiem*. These were not mere accoutrements of modernity imposed by foreign communities out of touch with local taste. The composer and pianist Alexander Tcherepnine — who was so taken with China that he cancelled the rest of a world tour and remained there for several years after 1934, marrying the pianist Lee Hsien Ming (Li Xianming) in 1938 — noted how his concerts always had a full house, and how audiences never made a sound and seemed to have an unusual capacity to concentrate. He became a professor at the Shanghai Conservatory, helping a generation of young composers to express their own local styles in modern forms; he was particularly amazed by how quick and easily his students caught on to modern music, unimpeded as they were by the earlier culture of classical music.[70] All these efforts resulted in world-class composers. Chou Wen-chung (Zhou Wenzhong), born in 1923, studied music in Shanghai from 1941–45, went to Boston from 1946 to 1949 where he studied with B. Martinu, using popular Chinese songs and modern composition, including atonal counterpoint. His *Landscapes* appeared in 1949, and he would compose many other stunning works of contemporary music in the United States, where he decided to stay after 1949. A protégé of Edgard Varèse, he stood out for combining the poetic traditions of native music with the highly sophisticated vocabulary of contemporary classical music, not unlike the work of Bela Bartók.

Jazz was so popular in China that Shanghai was seen as the jazz Mecca of Asia, as budding players from all over the world, as well as experienced players from the United States, tried out the seemingly endless venues for popular music. Buck Clayton, for instance, thought that Chinese appreciation of jazz in the 'Paris of the East' far outstripped the real Paris, and he also played popular native songs for local audiences during his two-year stay in the 1930s.[71] And jazz, just as classical music, was never simply copied locally: it was incorporated into new and inventive musical forms, combining Hollywood songs, jazz orchestration and local folk music on the pentatonic scale. These new forms of musical expression were immensely popular, with stars such as Zhou Xuan being broadcast over the radio and played on the gramophone, although they have yet to be studied in detail.[72] Unfortunately, the People's Republic did more than simply ban these popular forms of music after 1949: the great majority of the 80,000 records that were produced in the republican era and were deposited in a state archive after 1949 have been damaged beyond repair.[73]

It has long been recognised that one of the paradoxes of the republican period was the flourishing of literature and the arts in the midst of civil war and imperialist aggression: indeed, the May Fourth Movement is often celebrated as a key moment of enlightenment which left a positive legacy in an otherwise dark chapter of history. This book does not subscribe to the thematic centrality of this movement, and shows instead how historians have recently gone beyond May Fourth to show how pluralism, cosmopolitanism and, above all, openness were intrinsic to the era in a whole range of domains, from politics and religion to cinema and photography. Nor was openness confined to the intellectual elites of Shanghai and Beijing: a global outlook was promoted even in small local schools, while religious movements in the countryside were often explicitly engaged with global issues. Text, image and sound vehiculed knowledge of the foreign well beyond the main cities, while freedom of press, freedom of association and freedom of religion, even when severely curtailed, enhanced cultural diversity at all social levels. In the absence of a monopoly on power and knowledge, culture thrived, and so did a more open economy, as we see next.

# 5 Open Markets

A popular image, found for instance in John K. Fairbank's assertion that 'hostility toward alien things' characterised the Qing,[1] has it that foreign commodities were rejected by a xenophobic and self-sufficient empire. This is not the place to review the literature on the economic links forged with the rest of the world under the Qing: suffice it to say that the empire was not hermetically closed from the outside world, as a thriving maritime commerce allowed a range of goods, from cheap flints to expensive watches, to be imported, some of them being made available to large sections of the population. We should also note that a growing number of objects from abroad were copied at low cost to address the needs of a large but relatively poor population, a trend sustained by a long-standing tradition of manufacturing goods from foreign patterns, the use of component parts produced by individual workers in the assembly of complex objects, the spread of small enterprises in an expanding market from the sixteenth century onwards, and the availability of cheap labour because of a rapidly growing population. In short, already by the end of the nineteenth century, the everyday lives of a significant number of people in the empire were inextricably linked to global trends, from the yarn for clothes, the iron for tools or the oil in lamps for ordinary farmers to electric fans and imported phonographs in wealthy households.[2]

Our concern here, however, is with the first half of the twentieth century, and a number of important changes did occur to open up the movement of goods. As noted in Chapter 3, foreigners could build factories and manage workshops as a result of the Treaty of Shimonoseki signed at the end of the Sino-Japanese War in 1895. A spectacular burst of economic activity ensued in the following decade, as economic historians have noted. The readiness with which local merchants adopted modern technology, in particular after 1895, was remarkable. The scale of private investments also increased after the Sino-Japanese War, as not only merchants but also officials encouraged commercial activities which could help the country to recover rights to the exploitation of economic resources that had been lost to foreign companies.

The need for a legal basis for commerce and investment — crucial in opening up the economy — grew with the demand for greater capital in the years following the Shimonoseki Treaty, and culminated in the introduction of a Company Law in 1904. As David Faure shows, the balance of power between merchants and officials was overhauled: no longer was trade a privilege granted by imperial charter but a right for every citizen in return for tax.[3] The new law which gave recognition to company incorporation and limited liability was part of a broader shift towards a more open economy, as a Ministry of Commerce and chambers of commerce were created during the New Policies. Initiatives to open up the economy to foreign trade continued after 1911, one example being the fact that China was one of only ten countries in 1923 to sign an International Convention Relating to the Simplification of Customs Formalities, aimed at promoting international commerce by reducing excessive or arbitrary customs.[4] With these legal and institutional changes in mind, it is not surprising that the economy boomed in the first decades of the twentieth century, as the next section shows.

## Economic Growth

Research by economic historians has questioned the received idea that the economy regressed before 1949, that the incorporation of the country into a world economy led to the impoverishment of the vast majority of the population, that foreign companies benefited from special privileges which hindered the appearance of local enterprises, that foreign loans negotiated at extortionate rates crippled the country with debt, and that the absence of a strong central government prevented the emergence of a much needed infrastructure on which the local economy could develop. As a growing and substantial body of detailed research shows, this picture is no longer accepted by a majority of economic historians. While some have proposed just to modify this picture to take into account the positive indications of economic growth in the coastal regions of China, a number have undermined it altogether with detailed studies showing how the sustained increase of the output per head was the dominant feature of the economy until about 1930. And much of this economic growth was caused by the expansion of foreign trade.

Foreign trade in the second half of the nineteenth century may have disappointed merchants in the treaty ports, but it was important enough to have prompted Hao Yen-p'ing to write about a 'commercial revolution' during which local compradors and foreign entrepreneurs joined forces to pursue new opportunities created by free trade. Credit was eased with bills of exchange, the money supply grew with Mexican dollars and Chinese paper notes, the volume of trade expanded on international markets and global communications underwent a revolution, all these factors contributing to new synergies which were often dominated by local merchants: as much as 70 percent of all foreign shipping, for instance, may have been financed by local entrepreneurs.[5] The movement of goods was further facilitated by legal and economic reforms implemented from 1895 to 1904, as mentioned above, and the subsequent growth in international trade can easily be gauged from the data collected by the Maritime Customs under Robert Hart. The value of recorded trade excluding trade on local sailing vessels, for instance, grew from about 100,000 taels annually in the mid-1860s to 200,000 by the late 1880s to surpass 1 million during World War I. It continued to grow in the 1920s and reached a peak in 1931 at 3.24 million taels.[6] While opium was a major import in the nineteenth century, cotton goods took the largest share by 1900, although after 1911 the relative amount of chemicals, metals, petroleum and machinery gradually increased, while producer goods, used as inputs in the production of other products, exceeded cotton goods by 1931. Republican China exported large amounts of silk, tea and beans, although by the 1930s it also exported a whole range of manufactured products, including cotton goods. While the level of trade may not have been large when calculated on a per capita basis, given the enormous population, it was significant as a percentage of GDP rising from about 5 percent in the 1880s to 7–10 percent in the decades before 1937, some historians even calculating an average of 17 percent for the 1920s, although this figure may be inflated.[7]

While the overall amount of foreign trade was relatively modest for such a large country, it did have far-reaching consequences: as Thomas Rawski argues, free trade stimulated competition with imported goods, introduced new technologies and more resources into the economy, catalysed new local enterprises and attracted industry to coastal cities like Shanghai and Tianjin.[8] Local businesses, fired by foreign competition, used simple technologies involving low investment to concentrate on goods which were cheap and simple. Though often inferior to expensive imports, they responded to the needs of the vast masses of relatively poor people in China. Innovative enterprises appropriated foreign know-how in management, production and retail: they closely followed the lead of foreigners in the production of a huge number of items, ranging from matches and cigarettes to chemicals and machinery.[9] The appearance of enclaves under foreign administration in a number of treaty ports further accelerated the circulation of ideas, goods and people. Jack Gray has shown how the shipyards, public utilities and factories established in foreign concessions were training grounds for workers, managers and entrepreneurs alike: many went on to establish their own companies in the republican period.[10]

A concrete example of the impact of transfers of capital and technology can be found in the cotton industry. As cotton mills were established in China in the first decades of the twentieth century, machine-made cloth and yarn made rapid advances: the industry grew faster than anywhere else in the world, at times surpassing England and Japan in total output by the late 1920s. By 1934 an estimated three-quarters of available yarn was machine-made, meaning that even the cloth used by small households in remote parts of the country was based on an industrial product. Cloth also was increasingly manufactured by machine rather than by hand in the 1920s and 1930s: close to half of all production came from powerlooms rather than handlooms in 1936.[11] China even started exporting manufactured cloth, cotton pieces and factory yarn to overseas Chinese in Southeast Asia and more generally to the poor in Asia who demanded cheap goods: these items comprised a tenth of China's exports in value by 1936.[12] If we turn away from foreign trade alone and take into account the overall per capita gross domestic product, the effects of global integration become apparent: between 1912 and 1933 it grew from $113 to $123, although the population was increasing at a rate of at least 0.8 percent a year. During the same period modern industrial products, excluding those from Manchuria, grew over 6 percent per year, steamship tonnage by about 12 percent, railway mileage by over 10 percent, iron production by over 9 percent, coal by over 8 percent, and cotton yarn spindles by almost 12 percent.[13]

Innovations in money and finance did much to spread the positive impact of foreign trade on the economy as a whole. Only during the late Qing, for instance, was a special concession granted to operate a bank in accordance with modern practices: in 1897 the Imperial Bank of China in Shanghai, with a foreigner as Chief Manager, started issuing banknotes in the standard currency of taels. The tael notes issued by the bank greatly simplified business transactions, since it was much more convenient to deal in multidenominational banknotes than heavy and unwieldy metal currency in which other banks were still obliged to conduct business. Some fifty years later, after a major currency reform in 1935, there were over a hundred banks in the capital Chongqing alone, in addition to the four government banks and the Central Trust of China and the Postal Remittances and Savings Bank. In the territory controlled by the republican government, there were 293 private banks. The control and auditing of the banking system was strengthened from 1942 onwards with periodic inspections of books and accounts, although inflation ultimately undermine the entire economy.[14]

A Chinese Chartered Stock Exchange opened for business in September 1921 in Shanghai, the volume of business expanding rapidly and the daily turnover soon reaching a figure in excess of a million Chinese dollars.[15] Insurance companies, foreign and local, also thrived, and by 1927 the Insurance Association counted eighteen insurance companies. These made good progress during the years 1928–35, as members of the Insurance Association acquired re-insurance lines with foreign companies in order to be able to conduct business on the same basis and operate on equal terms: they started taking on the government's business such as railways, steamship lines and public warehouses.[16]

## The Countryside

Growth was not confined to the few treaty ports which benefited most from foreign trade: the rural economy boomed as well. Such is the reliance on negative assertions about the state of the economy that it is often forgotten that the opinions of contemporary observers were far more confident, including those who investigated the countryside in great detail. The most systematic, reliable and extensive sample survey of farmers was carried out by a University of Nanking team led by John L. Buck from 1929 to 1933. They surveyed in detail the entire population of 168 villages distributed over 22 provinces, collecting vast amounts of detailed information of the lives of over 16,000 farms. The results have been rejected by those supporting a more negative image of the typical 'Chinese peasant', although, as Jack Gray has pointed out, nothing in the methodology of the survey made positive conclusions inevitable.[17] *Land Utilization in China* scrupulously noted the many regional differences and varied forms of employment in the countryside, but the overall image which emerged from the study denied the existence of vast inequalities between rich landlords and impoverished tenants. Over half of all farmers were owners, many were part owners, and less than 6 percent were tenants. Most farms were relatively small, and very few were more than twice the average. Tenants were not generally much poorer than owners, since only fertile land could be rented out and increased income from small farms was made possible by a switch to crops which were more labour intensive and profitable on the market. In the south, for instance, tenants on irrigated rice land were better off than owners in the north, all the more since two grain crops could often be grown a year. A majority of farmers supplemented their incomes with handicrafts and other forms of non-agricultural employment from which 14 percent of their incomes were earned. One-third of all farmers surveyed were unaware of any adverse factors in agriculture, while none mentioned expensive credit, exploitative merchants or land tenure. Most, with the exception of farmers in the northwest, considered that their livelihoods had improved over the previous years: the voice of the farmer, as Gray points out, was a far cry from the revolutionary message of exploitation ceaselessly bandied about by the Communist Party.[18]

Economic historians have confirmed Buck's findings, as the average standard of living of most farmers improved steadily from 1870 to the early 1930s. Taxation may have been relatively high, but it became lighter, as average taxes rose less than prices until 1925.[19] Slow inflation from 1870 onwards was also beneficial to a majority of farmers since the cost of land and other agricultural expenses increased more slowly than the incomes that most countryside people received. The growth of agricultural production was particularly fast in central and east China between 1890 and 1930, and it may possibly have been twice as high as population growth: as a result of freedom of entry and exit and the mobility of capital and other resources, markets responded competitively to international prices and changes in the price of silver.[20]

More profitable crops also started to spread, for instance cotton, rape-seed, maize and sweet potatoes, while farmers profited from a greater circulation of new agricultural knowledge and techniques. One of the most valuable crops — opium — thrived again in the 1920s and 1930s despite official anti-opium legislation, the poppy providing an important impetus for the development of the local economy even if it was heavily taxed. While opium use has been decried by many historians, it was economically profitable to farmers: opium fields were labour-intensive, which suited regions with an abundant and cheap source of labour. Compact and light, the substance could be carried over great distances and could keep its quality over time, unlike more delicate crops such as rice and wheat, which presented storage problems as soon as they were harvested. Late nineteenth-century comparisons between the relative yields of wheat and poppy produced a profitability ratio of two to one in favour of the latter, explaining the popularity of opium in the countryside as a cash crop and export commodity. There was, however, a severe slump in the general economy in 1931–35 following the Great Depression in the United States: seventy years of growing prosperity for farmers came to an end. By 1935 the crisis subsided, and in 1936 growth resumed with a bumper harvest, although the war with Japan which started the following year and spiralling inflation in the 1940s would create havoc.[21]

The nature of the evidence about economic growth in the republican era is open to discussion, and the interpretation offered here, while based on a significant body of scholarship published by a number of distinguished economic historians, has by no means gained universal acceptance.[22] The point, however, is that of all the dimensions of republican history reviewed in this book, the economic record has generated more than enough scholarly debate for the negative view of 'economic imperialism' and 'economic collapse' to be all but discredited. Loren Brandt, Thomas Rawski, Jack Gray and David Faure, for instance, do not refute in their findings that there may have been increased economic disparities: they merely point out that overall, regardless of the relative gap between rich and poor, the average standard of living increased from 1870 to 1930.

It may never be possible to offer a definitive interpretation of the quantitative changes which took place in the republican economy, but different types of evidence are increasingly being offered in confirmation of this broadly positive picture. Besides calorie consumption, for instance, other indices of general health exist: rather than utilise scarce data for wages, movements in grain prices or output of cotton textiles to infer changes in the overall standard of living, Stephen L. Morgan has painstakingly assembled height data as a sensitive indicator of net nutrition for the twentieth century, which, as historians generally recognise, give a more precise measure of changes in welfare. Adding yet further evidence to the argument that the economy witnessed sustained growth for over half a century up till the outbreak of the Sino-Japanese War in 1937, his figures of physical stature show that most people grew taller up until the 1930s: on the other hand, there was hardly any improvement in final adult height between those born in the late 1920s (measured in the late 1940s) and the late 1970s (measured mid-1990s), which, to summarise a complex argument, indicates that World War II and the entire Maoist period was a nutritional setback for most people in China. Of course the sample on which Morgan's calculations are based is biased, like all samples, in this case because the subjects who underwent health screening tended to work in modern organisations in provinces along the coast. Nonetheless, it would seem that there was a modest rise in stature for most men and women from the 1890s to the 1930s.[23]

The slump from 1931 to 1935, while much less severe than the Great Depression in the United States and Europe from 1929 to 1939, attracted much of the negative press given to the role of foreign trade on China, in particular among nationalist writers who argued that the country was a semi-colony controlled by foreign powers. But the depression followed a long period of interaction with foreign trade which was directly responsible for the gradual increase of the standard of living in the countryside: 'it is hard to see another source of change in the early twentieth century that would have brought an impact on the rural economy as quickly and as effectively as an expansion of the market provided by international trade', in the words of David Faure.[24]

## Material Culture

Merely to point at the growing standard of living among many farming households is to miss the central argument of this book, namely that the first half of the twentieth century was a period of openness which allowed people, things and ideas to move in and out of the country as never before. While the 'dual economy' thesis, or the notion of a 'cellular economy of subsistence', according to which the rural economy remained unaffected by global flows while capitalism thrived in the cities along the coast, has long been discarded by economic historians,[25] it still holds sway among scholars who equate 'modernity' with 'urban'. But in contrast to other parts of the world such as Africa and South America, the material goods and technological innovations associated with foreign modernity were not merely imported for elite consumption: they were copied locally and quickly made available to much larger sections of the population. A two-tier economy appeared in which wealthy circles bought foreign goods and ordinary people welcomed cheap imitations, from the enamelled washbasin to the metal flashlight. A nationalist movement of import substitution in the first decades of the twentieth century further encouraged copy culture, easing the transformation of 'foreign goods' into 'national goods' within less than half a century. A relatively low intake of foreign goods — in contrast to Russia, the Ottoman Empire, South America, Africa and Southeast Asia — was not an indication of a lack of interest in things foreign, let alone 'hostility to alien things', but rather a measure of their success, as they were quickly appropriated and transformed into local products.[26]

Already before the collapse of the empire the majority of yarn used by rural households to make their clothes was produced by machines. Women of all social backgrounds selected scarves, skirts, blouses, gowns and corsets from a growing range of sartorial possibilities, using them in combinations which were often strikingly original: the use of the one-piece gown with a scarf and coat is but one example. In remote mountain villages, novel objects like imported clothes, shoes and hats (called Dutch hats by the farmers in Guangdong) were proudly paraded by the village elite in 1912, as the social restrictions on the conspicuous display of things modern dissipated with the fall of the empire.[27] By the end of the republican period even the very poor were likely to be wearing clothes spun from imported yarn, while a rickshaw puller could afford a cheap straw hat and shoes with rubber soles; the wealthy farmer, on the other hand, was proud to display his leather shoes and panama hat. Even when the gown retained its status among privileged circles, the suit became popular in the countryside, showing how ordinary people did not necessarily trail behind in the appropriation of material culture. The suit was so common that in a small market town near Chengdu no less than six tailors made them specifically for local people in 1942.[28] Where social elites sometimes preferred the more sombre hues dominant among the middle classes in Europe, ordinary people covered new surfaces in gay colours and adorned them with auspicious images, from enamelled plates to modern umbrellas.

Housing too was affected by the free flow of goods, technologies and knowledge: although wealthy merchants and government officials were often the first to transform their homes, glass remaining a luxury for decades, some new materials such as cement were relatively affordable even for the less privileged: in Shantou a stupendous number of new properties, valued at $50 million, were built of reinforced concrete in the 1920s.[29] And far from cosmopolitan cities such as Shanghai and Tianjin, returned emigrants built ostentatious mansions called 'foreign houses' in the villages of south Fujian and east Guangdong, incorporating new elements inspired from abroad, from the balcony to multiple floors, as well as local touches more in keeping with popular geomancy, like narrow windows warding off unpropitious forces. Thus houses not only materialised the social status of their owners but also incorporated their social cosmologies, new materials and new ideas allowing an enormous diversification of the architectural landscape in design, layout and substance.

While only minor changes appeared in the housing of the majority of poor farmers — one thinks of the use of corrugated iron in slums — many could afford at least a few new objects, none being more popular than the kerosene lamp, providing cheaper and better lighting. Such was the reach of kerosene that almost half of more than 200 localities scattered all over China reported in the early 1930s that their standard of living had increased thanks to the change from oil to kerosene lamps.[30] Rattan, more than any other material, popularised the easy chair. A passion for foreign clocks also transcended social barriers, many being hoarded in the imperial palace while much cheaper versions ticked away to the delighted wonder of humbler people.

Food is often seen as the aspect of daily life least permeable to foreign influence, China often being given as a prime example. Yet, during the republican era almost every aspect of food was changed by the inclusion of the country in a global economy which hugely expanded the existing culinary repertoire. Changes in diet were not restricted to the wealthy elites of the coastal cities: the very staple of food changed in taste and aspect, as rice, sugar and wheat were increasingly produced industrially, white being the desired colour. Simple objects like the thermos flask and enamelware transformed the material culture of food, while those with a little money to spare might experience 'foreign' food — by a visit to a simple stall on the pavement or a lavishly decorated exotic restaurant with a menu in a strange language. Moreover, the use of tins enormously expanded the range of available foodstuffs, whether simple dishes or rare delicacies, across regions and seasons, for rich and poor alike. Cultural bricolage pervaded every aspect of life, including creative appropriations in the kitchen, as dishes now considered quintessentially 'Chinese' made their first appearance in the thriving culinary environment of the republican period — fried egg with tomato being a prime example. Bread, ice-cream and yoghurt became popular, sold by peddlers on the street, while 'Western' restaurants could be found in most cities by the start of World War II. Several hundred emerged in Shanghai alone, more than thirty vied for customers in Canton, and a dozen catered for the social and political elites of Tianjin.[31] In Chongqing foreign food could be found all over the city.[32] As in England and France, studied by Stephen Mennell,[33] the trend in modern China was towards a more varied experience in eating and more varied tastes — thanks to the advent of manufactured foods and the closer integration of the country with a global economy.[34]

A more open market thus enormously increased the range of affordable goods: even in impoverished Zouping, Shandong province, hundreds of items from the factories in Qingdao, Shanghai, Tianjin, Japan, Europe and the United States were on offer, heightening choice and lowering costs. Another example is Zhonghechang, a small market town of 15,000 farmers in rural Sichuan, where on market days simple stalls offered a range of new goods by the 1940s, from soap, towels, cream, powder and rouge to spectacles — not counting a dozen shops dealing exclusively in luxury items. In short, even if disposable income grew only slowly in the countryside, it bought many more varied objects than ever before. The availability of cheap machines, on the other hand, allowed a handicraft system in the countryside to be consolidated, as raw material was more easily transformed by small groups of workers into finished goods. After 1949, on the other hand, a command economy would reduce choice to a few items produced in state-owned urban enterprises run without much regard for consumers, who found that most of them were reject products needing to be frequently repaired or replaced altogether. A measure of diversity was introduced only after 1979, although the economy remained dominated by large and generally wasteful state enterprises.

## Transportation

The failure of central government to provide an effective transportation system has been deplored by some historians of the republican era: the military control of railways, already inadequate by international standards, adversely affected the free flow of goods, roads outside the foreign concessions were all but inexistent and lack of adequate governance meant that people moved on foot or by cart or boat. This image has not been significantly altered by recent research, which has tended to concentrate on the politics behind modern transportation, for instance the rivalry between steamship companies or international involvement in railway construction. However, as we have seen in Chapter 2, underneath the many power struggles in Beijing, several of the ministries created by the New Policies worked rather effectively throughout the republican era. We have already mentioned the Ministry of Justice and the Foreign Ministry, but the Ministry of Communications in charge of the railways, telegraph and postal services also functioned professionally despite a sometimes hostile political environment. Resources were poured into the ministry for constructing railways and extending the telegraph system, and it was dominated by competent and powerful officials with influence in the world of banking.[35] Contemporary travellers, both local and foreign, believed that they were in the middle of a genuine revolution in transportation, and their impressions are corroborated by evidence generally ignored by historians keen to portray the republican era in a negative light.

By the end of the 1920s, for instance, reports from all over the country told of new roads being energetically and enthusiastically built, 'roads which are levelling the walls and entirely changing the face of old Chinese cities, roads running along the banks of rivers, winding in and out of villages, even climbing over mountain passes'.[36] A chemist based at West China Union University, William Sewell was startled in the 1930s by the rapid changes which were taking place, as hundreds of cars and lorries were imported, rickshaws, bicycles and cars replaced wheelbarrows, sedan chairs and rumbling wooden carts, while even the camel caravans of northern deserts were threatened by tractors with caterpillar wheels: 'Crooked and narrow ways and winding, evil-smelling alleys are swallowed up in the fine straight roads, so that a traveller returning after a few months' absence can scarcely find his home.'[37] Victor Purcell, keen observer of local life and experienced explorer, expressed his astonishment at the 'remarkable achievement' of the road system, which had been virtually non-existent in the 1920s; even relatively remote cities like Nanning, Liuzhou and Guilin in Guangxi province had wide concrete streets lined with trees.[38]

Even if cars were relatively rare, new networks of buses regularly plied in the city and the countryside by the 1930s. In Beijing a hundred buses ran daily in the early 1930s, easily competing with the camel caravans which were still a common sight relished by foreign tourists.[39] As Dudley Buxton noted in his human geography published in 1929, the old order was changing rapidly and motorbuses were reaching as far as into Sichuan.[40] Peter Fleming, intrepid traveller who did not hesitate to trek off the beaten path by every means possible, elegantly captured the advantages of the bus over the train: 'The bus service, as a Chinese institution, is both conceived and carried out on a far sounder basis than the railway. It requires a much smaller capital outlay, and therefore presents fewer opportunities for squeeze. A road is quicker as well as cheaper to build than a railway, and the Chinese talent for delay is accordingly a less operative factor. The running of a bus service, as compared with the running of a railway, is not only easier but offers more scope for individualism, and is therefore better suited to the Chinese character. Finally, in the event of political upheavals, a bus service is less vulnerable than a railway because its capital value is much smaller.'[41] Buses went where railways failed to penetrate, giving unprecedented freedom of movement to millions, as they allowed persons, goods and ideas to find their way into the interior, integrating local economies into a national and global network of interdependent links.

Cheap travel abroad became possible already in the second half of the nineteenth century thanks to the steamer, as a migrant could make his way from Xiamen to Manila for a few dollars in 1884.[42] The majority of passengers were poor and travelled on deck. When Gong Debo (1891–1980) took a trip by steamboat from Hankou to Shanghai and thence to Japan as an impoverished student, he expressed his delight at the speed, comfort and economy of modern travel, which he contrasted to the slow junks which plied the waterways in his native Hunan.[43] Even death was an object moved more gracefully thanks to the steamer. Coffins travelled widely with new means of transportation, and large international liners would invariably bear two or three coffins from overseas Chinese;[44] several hundred were sent to Hong Kong every year from all over the world in the 1920s and 1930s, en route to their ancestral villages.[45]

Like the bus and the steamer, the train allowed people and goods to be carried at greater speed to more distant places. While it is true that the railway services suffered from intermittent if not complete interruption for months on end during the Beiyang government — commandeering locomotives and rolling stock at will — a marked improvement appeared in the late 1920s,[46] while considerable sections were added in the 1930s. On the eve of the Sino-Japanese war, a 420-km gap in the Canton-Hankou line was bridged, thus enabling passengers to use a route from Hong Kong via Canton and

Changsha to Hankou, and for a brief period even to Beijing, Manchuria and across Siberia to Europe: known as the Hong Kong-Calais line, it was the longest continuous rail route in the world. Wang Fuming has shown that farmers used new opportunities provided by international trade and new transportation to produce on a large scale for outside markets. Thanks to the railway, enterprising boys as young as fourteen or fifteen left their villages in Hebei province to find better-paid jobs as far away as Manchuria.[47] By 1933 over 10,000 km covered some 19 provinces and transported 45 million passengers annually; as the historian Chang Jui-te has recently indicated, the fact that all new railways were constructed by local engineers and managed by local experts was an 'outstanding achievement' indicating how, despite a climate dominated by military concerns, professional standards were rapidly and successfully promoted by successive republican governments.[48]

Planes are rarely mentioned in accounts of the republican period, even if China enthusiastically participated in the growth of aeronautics. A mere three years after Louis Blériot flew across the English Channel, Zee Yee Lee not only obtained an aviator's certificate in England, but also brought back two Etrich monoplanes equipped with Austro-Daimler engines in 1911. He voluntarily presented the two planes to the government, which he joined under Sun Yatsen, becoming the first Chinese aviator and the head of the first government Aviation Department.[49] The first aerial mail passenger service was inaugurated on 7 May 1920 between Beijing and Tianjin, and in 1929 an American company known as Aviation Exploration pioneered China's first regular airline under a franchise issued by the Ministry of Communications. Its name changed to China Airways and a contract was signed with the government in July 1930, providing for the joint establishment of the China National Aviation Corporation which developed a nationwide network of air mail and passenger services. Shanghai, Hankou, Beijing, Canton and Hong Kong: by 1937 the airline company provided a regular service on some 5,000 km of air routes for 15,000 passengers.[50]

The Southwest Aviation Corporation, a purely local enterprise subsidised by the provincial governments of Guangxi and Guangdong in Canton, appeared in 1932 while the Eurasia Aviation Company, two-thirds owned by the Chinese government and one-third by Deutsche Lufthansa, started a service from Shanghai to Beijing and to Manchuria in 1931 on German planes; Russian airlines then transported mail and passengers on to Moscow, Lufthansa flying the final leg to Berlin: China's airlines were by then truly international. Chengdu and Kunming were also integrated into the national network, as airlines were unable to keep up with ever-increasing demand for service: travel by air was not only faster but actually cheaper than by land, as fares averaged about 10 cents a mile. Even excess baggage was assessed at rates cheap enough to encourage merchants to explore new markets in the interior and supply shipments entirely by air. Transport by air over areas affected by flood, famine and banditry was comfortable and secure. Freight services grew phenomenally after the war, as planes were block-booked by merchants to fly commercial goods and perishable foods across the country.[51]

While movement by cart or boat in China around 1900 generally proceeded at a walking pace, a revolution in transportation in the following decades meant that people across the social spectrum could move faster, further and cheaper than ever before. Trains may have been shabbily equipped and poorly heated, but they too were always crowded, passengers spilling over into the corridors and on to the roof. The most common means of motorised transportation for ordinary farmers in the hinterland, however, was probably the bus, even if windows were broken and progress was uneven on the poorly macadamised roads of republican China. In all cases new distribution points were created for foreign goods, more resources were opened up, much closer territorial integration was achieved, longer and safer voyages were made possible, and a denser network was shaped that stretched out far beyond the country to the rest of the world. While much of the machinery might have seemed woefully inadequate to some foreigners, new modes of transportation were generally welcomed by a population keen to profit from quicker and cheaper movement. Some owners of houses demolished without compensation may have been resentful of road building, but overall there is little evidence to support the image of a 'xenophobic rejection' of machinery, a 'fear of the mechanical' or 'cultural estrangement' in the face of modernity. For people of very different backgrounds machinery stood for modernity, whether in the eyes of farmers taking their chicken to market in dilapidated buses or among the polyglot elites crisscrossing the country by train and plane.[52]

# 6 Conclusion

*Glasnost* in the Soviet Union, *kaifang* in China or *doi moi* in Vietnam: 'openness' in socialist states has become such an inflated term of political propaganda that one tends to forget that prerevolutionary regimes were often marked by a much higher degree of cosmopolitanism. In Russia, as Jeffrey Brooks reminds us, the Bolsheviks inherited an empire in which not only political elites were in tune with the rest of Europe and the United States, but the newly literate farmers sought out an increasingly cosmopolitan culture in film and fiction, while foreign models dominated in politics, the economy was open to the world and international practice was accommodated in fields ranging from corporate banking to human rights.[1] In the case of China, as this book has argued, the period from 1900 to 1949 was characterised by engagement with the world at all levels of society, and the pursuit of openness was particularly evident in four areas, namely in governance and the advance of the rule of law and of newly acquired liberties; in freedom of movement in and out of the country; in open minds thriving on ideas from the humanities and sciences; and in open markets and sustained growth in the economy. The era between empire and communism is routinely portrayed as a catastrophic interlude in the country's modern history, but this book, built on the strength of a growing secondary literature, indicates instead that while there is always a pull between closure and openness in all societies at all times, the extent and depth of engagement with the rest of the world was such that we can see closure under Mao instead as the exception. As in Russia under Stalin, China under Mao witnessed the disintegration of international links in economics, politics and culture, a gradual closure of minds which constituted a radical reversal in everyday experience rather than the continuation of a long tradition. Why this happened is a question which transcends the limits of this book: after all, communists in the republican era profited as much if not more than others from an open environment, from shopping for military hardware in Shanghai and training abroad to receiving extensive assistance from Soviet advisors.

If the Maoist period is an aberration rather than the gravity point in the modern history of China, could we go a step further and instead of interpreting the last two or three centuries as a tale of unstoppable progress towards 'revolution', from the 'Opium Wars' to the 'Cultural Revolution', see it as an unfolding embrace of the world, an intensification of global connectivity, a gradual increase in the flow of people, goods, ideas, institutions and techniques? This approach would certainly be supported by new evidence about the imperial period, as a number of historians increasingly argue in favour of a secular trend towards openness which would have started many centuries ago. In *The Open Empire*, for instance, Valerie Hansen depicts the country as dynamic, vibrant and open to outside influences throughout its history rather than as a hermit kingdom indifferent to foreign lands.[2] Joanna Waley-Cohen, too, highlights how there was a longstanding tradition of extensive interaction with the outside world: it was not so much splendid isolation which was pursued throughout the country's long history, but ideas, goods and techniques from outside, ranging from the 'early cosmopolitanism' of the Han and the Tang to the Ming and Qing's fascination with science, technology and astronomy from Europe.[3] The empire energetically engaged with the rest of the world, often encouraging the circulation of foreign goods and ideas — in contrast to the hoary stereotype of a xenophobic China opposed to all things foreign.

Even if we debunk the myth of a monolithic empire ensconced behind its walls in favour of a more nuanced approach which highlights the many global connections established by a multicultural empire during the last centuries of its existence, the first half of the twentieth century saw a qualitatively unprecedented intensification of this trend towards openness. Freedom of association, freedom to travel, freedom of religion, freedom to trade and relative freedom of speech, as we have seen, wrought profound changes in the texture of everyday life, from the appearance of huge metropoles to a lively press, while the introduction of the rule of law, constitutional government, democratic elections and oppositional politics constituted an extraordinary transformation of the realm of politics. Participatory politics may very well have been coupled with what appeared to be political instability in the eyes of observers who favoured firm rule from above, just as exposure to international commerce could cause the periodic financial instabilities deplored by proponents of trade protection, but the sheer depth and scale of engagement with the rest of the world was without precedent. And globalisation, as this book has argued, was a vector of cultural diversification, which, in turn, was best supported by increased globalisation: pre-existing constellations of ideas, practices and institutions did not simply vanish on contact with the rest of the world, but on the contrary expanded and diversified even further, just as much as local industries diversified thanks to their inclusion into a much larger global market. We have seen how voluntary associations boomed, newspapers and magazines flourished, intellectual activities burgeoned, foreign communities grew and material culture was enriched, leading to ever more complex and rapidly shifting social and cultural arrangements, in turn enhanced by elements of political pluralism. Arguably the country was at its most diverse in its entire history on the eve of World War II — in terms of politics, society, culture and economy.

If openness is a key characteristic of the country's long history of engagement with the rest of the world, can we interpret the 'Open Door' policy since 1978 as a return to a tradition of engagement with the world? The most common reservation is that the recent overture of markets and minds has not been matched by political reform, as the party leadership has repeatedly rejected the need for democratic practices and proclaimed the superiority of a system based on communist rule: with vigorous economic growth these views are unlikely to be substantially altered. The optimistic interpretation, however, argues that increased interdependence with the rest of the world might eventually lead to participatory politics and the rule of law, while on the other hand the pessimistic view points at the use of a relative degree of economic openness to shore up the power of a privileged elite at the expense of the civil liberties of ordinary people. Whatever the case may be, the overlooked cosmopolitan experience of the republican era is of even greater relevance today, now that even in the People's Republic globalisation rather than revolution has become the guiding issue for the twenty-first century.

# Notes

## Chapter 1

1   The focus of this short study is the period from 1911 to 1949, usually referred to as republican China, but frequent mention is made of the New Policies initiated after the defeat of the Boxer Rebellion in 1900 and the reforms which followed in the wake of the 1895 Shimonoseki peace settlement: the era from 1895 to 1949 I loosely refer to as 'modern China'.

2   An early call against teleology and the 'revolution paradigm' appeared in a remarkable article by Ramon H. Myers and Thomas A. Metzger, 'Sinological shadows: The state of modern China studies in the United States', *Australian Journal of Chinese Affairs*, no. 4 (July 1980), pp. 1–34; the counterpart of the 'revolution paradigm' is the notion of a 'Western impact', seen to have triggered the beginning of the revolution as China entered an 'era of collapse', and on this one should read P. A. Cohen, *Discovering history in China: American historical writing on the recent Chinese past*, New York: Columbia University Press, 1984; on the recent historiography of modern China, helpful is Rana Mitter, 'Historiographical review: Modernity, internationalization, and war in the history of modern China', *Historical Journal*, 48, no. 2 (2005), pp. 523–43.

3   Sugata Bose, 'Starvation amidst plenty: The making of famine in Bengal, Honan and Tonkin, 1942–45', *Modern Asian Studies*, 24, no. 4 (Oct. 1990), p. 700.

4   Fu Zhengyuan, *Autocratic tradition and Chinese politics*, Cambridge University Press, 1993, reviewed by Roger B. Jeans in the *China Quarterly*, no. 143 (Sept. 1995), p. 878.

## Chapter 2

1   Arthur Waldron, 'The warlord: Twentieth-century Chinese understandings of violence, militarism, and imperialism', *The American Historical Review*, 96, no. 4 (Oct. 1991), pp. 1073–1100.

2   Jean Chesneaux, 'The federalist movement in China, 1920–1923', in Jack Gray (ed.), *Modern China's search for a political form*, Oxford University Press, 1969, p. 108; see also Li Dajia, *Minguo chunian de liansheng zizhi yundong* (The federalist movement in early republican China), Taipei: Hongwenguan chubanshe, 1984.

3   Arthur Waldron, 'Warlordism versus federalism: The revival of a debate?', *The China Quarterly*, no. 121 (March 1990), pp. 116–28.

4   Leslie H. Dingyan Chen, *Chen Jiongming and the federalist movement: Regional leadership and nation building in early republican China*, Ann Arbor: University of Michigan Press, 1999.

5   R. Keith Schoppa, 'Province and nation: The Chekiang Provincial Autonomy Movement, 1917–1927', *Journal of Asian Studies*, 36, no. 4 (Aug. 1977), pp. 661–74.

6   James A. Millward, *Beyond the pass: Economy, ethnicity, and empire in Qing Central Asia, 1759–1864*, Stanford University Press, 1998; Peter C. Perdue, *China marches west: The Qing conquest of central Eurasia*, Cambridge, MA: Belknap Press, 2005.

7   Ch'en Ts'un-kong, *Lieqiang dui Zhongguo de junhuo jinyun: Min guo 8 nian — 18 nian* (The foreign powers' arms embargo against China from 1919 to 1929), Taipei: Zhongyang yanjiuyuan jindaishi yanjiusuo, 1983.

8   Thomas Rawski, *Economic growth in prewar China*, Berkeley: University of California Press, 1989, p. 39.

9   Ibid., p. 40.

10   Arthur Waldron, *From war to nationalism: China's turning point, 1924–1925*, Cambridge University Press, 1995.

11   Rawski, *Economic growth in prewar China*, p. 37.

12   Ibid., p. 42.

13   Tien Hung-mao, *Government and politics in Kuomintang China, 1927–1937*, Stanford University Press, 1972, pp. 138 and 143.

14   Qin Shao, *Culturing modernity: The Nantong Model, 1890–1930*, Stanford University Press, 2004; Lenore Barkan, 'Patterns of power: Forty years of elite politics in a Chinese county', in Joseph W. Esherick and Mary B. Rankin (eds.), *Chinese local elites and patterns of dominance*, Berkeley: University of California Press, 1990, pp. 191–215; on the transformation of the material landscape in republican China, including the building of roads and electrification, see Frank Dikötter, *Exotic commodities: Modern objects and everyday life in China*, New York: Columbia University Press, 2007.

15   Harold S. Quigley, 'Federalism and foreign relations in China', *Political Science Quarterly*, 42, no. 4 (Dec. 1927), pp. 561–70.

16   Harold S. Quigley, 'Aspects of China's constitutional problem', *Political Science Quarterly*, 39, no. 2 (June 1924), p. 198.

17  Frank Dikötter, *Crime, punishment and the prison in modern China*, New York: Columbia University Press, 2002.

18  John H. Fincher, *Chinese democracy: The self-government movement in local, provincial and national politics, 1905–1914*, London: Croom Helm, 1981, p. 219.

19  See Douglas R. Reynolds, *China, 1898–1912: The* xinzheng *revolution and Japan*, Cambridge, MA: Harvard University Press, 1993.

20  Roger R. Thompson, 'The lessons of defeat: Transforming the Qing state after the Boxer War', *Modern Asian Studies*, 37, no. 4 (Oct. 2003), p. 771.

21  *Report of the Commission on Extra-Territoriality in China*, London: HM Stationery Office, 1926, Cmd. 2774, pp. 79, 92–4.

22  Dikötter, *Crime, punishment and the prison in modern China*.

23  J. B. Condliffe, *China to-day: Economic*, Boston: World Peace Foundation, 1932, p. 117.

24  Dikötter, *Crime, punishment and the prison in modern China*.

25  Julia C. Strauss, *Strong institutions in weak polities: State building in republican China, 1927–1940*, New York: Oxford University Press, 1998.

26  Elizabeth J. Remick, *Building local states: China during the republican and post-Mao eras*, Cambridge, MA: Harvard University Press, 2004.

27  Prasenjit Duara, *Culture, power, and the state: Rural north China, 1900–1942*, Stanford University Press, 1988.

28  Edmund S. K. Fung, *In search of Chinese democracy: Civil opposition in nationalist China, 1929–1949*, Cambridge University Press, 2000.

29  Mark Elvin, 'The gentry democracy in Chinese Shanghai, 1905–1914', in Jack Gray (ed.), *Modern China's search for a political form*, Oxford University Press, 1969, pp. 41–66.

30  Roger R. Thompson, *China's local councils in the age of constitutional reform, 1898–1911*, Cambridge, MA: Harvard University Press, 1995.

31  Fincher, *Chinese democracy*, pp. 270–1.

32  Louise Edwards, *Gender, politics and democracy: Women's suffrage in China*, Stanford University Press, 2008.

33  Chesneaux, 'The federalist movement in China, 1920–1923', pp. 107–8.

34  See Roger B. Jeans (ed.), *Roads not taken: The struggle of opposition parties in twentieth-century China*, Boulder, CO: Westview Press, 1992; see also Eugene Lubot, *Liberalism in an illiberal age: New Culture liberals in republican China, 1919–1937*, Westport, CN: Greenwood Press, 1982; Marina Svensson, *Debating human rights in China: A conceptual and political history*, Lanham: Rowman and Littlefield, 2002.

35  Fung, *In search of Chinese democracy*, pp. 346–7.

36  Sidney D. Gamble, *North China villages: Social, political, and economic activities before 1933*, Berkeley: University of California Press, 1963, pp. 41–2, 151–2, 167–9.

37 'On the eve of the China People's Conference', *Pacific Affairs*, 4, no. 6 (June 1931), pp. 527–9.

38 John A. Fairlie, 'Constitutional developments in China', *The American Political Science Review*, 25, no. 4 (Nov. 1931), pp. 1016–22.

39 Guenther Stein, 'People's Political Council reorganizing', *Far Eastern Survey*, 11, no. 14 (July 1942), pp. 158–60.

40 Fung, *In search of Chinese democracy*.

41 A. Doak Barnett, *China on the eve of communist takeover*, New York: Praeger, 1963, pp. 60–70.

42 Chen Chih-mai, 'Post-war government of China', *The Journal of Politics*, 9, no. 4 (Nov. 1947), pp. 503–21.

43 Thomas E. Greiff, 'The principle of human rights in nationalist China: John C. H. Wu and the ideological origins of the 1946 Constitution', *The China Quarterly*, no. 103 (Sept. 1985), p. 446.

44 Carl Crow, *China takes her place*, New York: Harper, 1944, p. v.

45 Fincher, *Chinese democracy*, p. 266.

46 Min-ch'ien Tuk Zug Tyau, *China awakened*, New York: Macmillan, 1922, pp. 116–7.

47 Andrew J. Nathan, *Chinese democracy*, New York: Knopf, 1985, pp. 145–8; on foreign languages in the religious periodical press, see Rudolph Löwenthal, *The religious periodical press in China*, Beijing: Synodal Commission in China, 1940, p. 281.

48 See, for instance, Xu Xiaoqun, *Chinese professionals and the republican state: The rise of professional associations in Shanghai, 1912–1937*, Cambridge University Press, 2001.

49 Li Shijie, 'Sixing zhi yanjiu' (Research on the death penalty), *Jianyu zazhi*, 1, no. 1 (Nov. 1929), pp. 1–6.

50 Tyau, *China awakened*, p. 121.

51 Stephen R. MacKinnon, 'Toward a history of the Chinese press in the republican period', *Modern China*, 23, no. 1 (Jan. 1997), pp. 3–32.

52 Ibid., p. 18.

53 L. Sophia Wang, 'The independent press and authoritarian regimes: The case of the *Dagong bao* in republican China', *Pacific Affairs*, 67, no. 2 (summer 1994), pp. 216–41.

54 Fincher, *Chinese democracy*, p. 255.

55 Olga Lang, *Chinese family and society*, New Haven: Yale University Press, 1946, p. 91.

56 William T. Rowe, *Hankow: Conflict and community in a Chinese city*, Stanford University Press, 1989; Mary B. Rankin, *Elite activism and political transformation in China, Zhejiang province, 1865–1911*, Stanford University Press, 1986.

57 Marianne Bastid, 'Currents of social change' in D. Twitchett and J.K.

Fairbank (eds.), *The Cambridge history of China*, Cambridge University Press, 1980, vol. 11, part 2, pp. 562–3.

58 Chinese Ministry of Information, *China handbook, 1937–1945: A comprehensive survey of major developments in China in eight years of war*, New York: Da Capo Press, 1947, p. 589.

59 Marie-Claire Bergère, *The golden age of the Chinese bourgeoisie, 1911–1937*, Cambridge University Press, 1989, p. 57; see also Liu Zehua and Liu Jianqing, 'Civic associations, political parties, and the cultivation of citizenship consciousness in modern China', in Joshua A. Fogel and Peter G. Zarrow (eds.), *Imagining the people: Chinese intellectuals and the concept of citizenship, 1890–1920*, Armonk, NY: Sharpe, 1997, pp. 39–60.

60 Tyau, *China awakened*, p. 159.

61 David Strand, 'Historical perspectives' in Deborah Davis, Richard Kraus, Barry Naughton and Elizabeth Perry (eds.), *Urban spaces in contemporary China*, Cambridge University Press, 1995, p. 419.

62 David Strand, *Rickshaw Beijing: City people and politics in the 1920s*, Berkeley: University of California Press, 1989, p. 177.

63 Ibid., p. 285; see also Mary B. Rankin, 'State and society in early republican politics, 1912–18', *China Quarterly*, no. 150 (June 1997), pp. 271–3.

64 Robert J. Culp, 'Elite association and local politics in republican China: Educational institutions in Jiashan and Lanqi Counties, Zhejiang, 1911–1937', *Modern China*, 20, no. 4 (Oct. 1994), pp. 446–77.

65 Elizabeth VanderVen, 'Village-state cooperation: Modern community schools and their funding, Haicheng County, Fengtian, 1905–1931', *Modern China*, 31, no. 2 (April 2005), pp. 204–35.

66 See Caroline Reeves, 'The power of mercy: The Chinese Red Cross Society, 1900–1937', doctoral dissertation, Harvard University, 1998, and Shirley S. Garrett, *Social reformers in urban China: The Chinese Y.M.C.A., 1895–1926*, Cambridge, MA: Harvard University Press, 1970.

67 Léon Vandermeersch, 'An enquiry into the Chinese conception of the law', in Stuart R. Schram, *The scope of state power in China*, London: School of Oriental and African Studies, 1985, pp. 3–26; see also William C. Jones, 'Chinese law and liberty in comparative historical perspective', in William C. Kirby (ed.), *Realms of freedom in modern China*, Stanford University Press, 2004, pp. 44–56.

68 See, among others, William C. Kirby, 'China unincorporated: Company law and business enterprise in twentieth-century China', *Journal of Asian Studies*, 54, no. 1 (Feb. 1995), pp. 43–63.

69 Dikötter, *Crime, punishment and the prison in modern China*; see also Alison Conner, 'Lawyers and the legal profession during the republican period',

in Kathryn Bernhardt and Philip C. C. Huang (eds.), *Civil Law in Qing and republican China*, Stanford University Press, 1994, pp. 215–48.

70 Sifayuan (ed.), *Quanguo sifa huiyi huibian* (Documents on the national judiciary conference), Nanjing: Sifayuan, 1935; see also J. E. Lemière, 'La première conférence judiciaire chinoise', *Revue Nationale Chinoise*, 23, no. 77 (14 Oct. 1935), pp. 165–75.

71 Laszlo Ladany, *Law and legality in China: The testament of a China-watcher*, London: Hurst, 1992, pp. 49–50.

72 Meredith P. Gilpatrick, 'The status of law and lawmaking procedure under the Kuomintang 1925–46', *The Far Eastern Quarterly*, 10, no. 1 (Nov. 1950), p. 54.

# Chapter 3

1 On this, see some interesting comments by J. R. Levenson, *Revolution and cosmopolitanism: The Western stage and the Chinese stages*, Berkeley: University of California Press, 1971.

2 Michael R. Godley, 'The late Ch'ing courtship of the Chinese in Southeast Asia', *The Journal of Asian Studies*, 34, no. 2 (Feb. 1975), pp. 361–85; to put this in comparative perspective, a similar number of emigrants from South Asia would only be reached by the end of the twentieth century; see Judith M. Brown (ed.), *Global South Asians: Introducing the modern diaspora*, Cambridge University Press, 2006.

3 Wang Gungwu, *The Chinese overseas: From earthbound China to the quest for autonomy*, Cambridge, MA: Harvard University Press, 2000, p. 40.

4 Wu Lien-teh, *Plague fighter: The autobiography of a modern Chinese physician*, Cambridge: Heffer, 1959.

5 Lee Guan-kin, 'Responding to eastern and western cultures in Singapore: A comparative study of Khoo Seok Wan, Lim Boon Keng and Song Ong Siang', doctoral dissertation, University of Hong Kong, 1997.

6 Lee, 'Responding to eastern and western cultures in Singapore'.

7 'Report on the trade of Amoy, for the year 1883', *Report on the trade at the ports of China for the year 1883*, Shanghai: Imperial Maritime Customs' Press, 1884, p. 294.

8 'Report on the trade of Kiungchow, for the year 1893', *Report on the trade at the ports of China for the year 1893*, Shanghai: Imperial Maritime Customs' Press, 1894, p. 551.

9 Hu Zijin, 'Guangzhou zhuzhici' (Bamboo verses on Canton) in Lei Mengshui *et al.* (eds.), *Zhonghua zhuzhici* (Bamboo verses of China), Beijing: Beijing guji chubanshe, 1997, vol. 4, p. 2897.

10 D. S. Hosie, *Portrait of a Chinese lady*, London: Hodder and Stoughton, 1929, p. 58.

11 'Wuchow', *Decennial reports, 1922–31*, Shanghai: Statistical Department of the Inspectorate General of Customs, 1933, p. 279.

12 Zhu Huayu, *Huaqiao shehui shenghuo yu jiaoyu* (Social life and education of overseas Chinese), Canton: Huaqiao wenti yanjiushe, 1937, pp. 114–7.

13 'Report on the trade of Amoy, for the year 1904', *Report on the trade at the ports of China for the year 1904*, Shanghai: Imperial Maritime Customs' Press, 1905, p. 648; 'Report on the trade of Amoy, for the year 1908', *Report on the trade at the ports of China for the year 1908*, Shanghai: Imperial Maritime Customs' Press, 1909, p. 480.

14 Chen Da, *Nanyang huaqiao yu Min Yue shehui* (Overseas Chinese from Southeast Asia and society in Fujian and Guangdong), Shanghai: Shangwu yinshuguan, 1938; see also Liu Shimu and Xu Zhigui, *Huaqiao gaiguan* (General survey of overseas Chinese), Shanghai: Zhonghua shuju, 1935, pp. 50–3.

15 Chen, *Nanyang huaqiao yu Min Yue shehui*, p. 116.

16 Ibid., p. 120.

17 Chen Ta, *Chinese migrations, with special reference to labor conditions*, Washington, DC: Government Printing Office, 1923, p. 157.

18 Stephen Fitzgerald, *China and the overseas Chinese: A study of Peking's changing policy*, Cambridge University Press, 1972, pp. 121–2.

19 See the essential work of John M. Carroll, *Edge of empires: Chinese elites and British colonials in Hong Kong*, Cambridge, MA: Harvard University Press, 2005.

20 Ng Lun Ngai-Ha, 'The role of Hong Kong educated Chinese in the shaping of modern China', *Modern Asian Studies*, 17, no. 1 (1983), pp. 137–63.

21 Priscilla Roberts, 'Paul D. Cravath and China between the wars', *Tamkang Journal of International Affairs*, 4, no. 1 (fall 1999), pp. 31–2.

22 Diran John Sohigian, 'The life and times of Lin Yutang', doctoral dissertation, New York: Columbia University, 1991, p. 668.

23 Kingsley Bolton, *Chinese Englishes: A sociolinguistic history*, Cambridge University Press, 2003, pp. 243–4.

24 Margaret E. Burton, *Notable women of modern China*, New York: Revell, 1912, pp. 115–220; G. H. Choa, *'Heal the sick' was their motto: The Protestant medical missionaries in China*, Hong Kong: Chinese University Press, 1990, pp. 81–2.

25 Eric Teichman, *Travels of a consular officer in north-west China*, Cambridge University Press, 1921, pp. 116–7; see also Robert S. Clark and Arthur de Carle Sowerby, *Through Shen-kan: The account of the Clark Expedition in north China 1908–9*, London: Fisher Unwin, 1912, p. 62.

26 Albert Feuerwerker, *The foreign establishment in China in the early twentieth century*, Ann Arbor: University of Michigan Press, 1976, p. 38.

27   Min-ch'ien Tuk Zug Tyau, *China awakened*, New York: Macmillan, 1922, pp. 222–3; see also Julean Arnold, *China: A commercial and industrial handbook*, Washington, DC: Government Printing Office, 1926, p. 66, and Edward T. Williams, *China yesterday and to-day*, London: George Harrap, 1923, p. 581.

28   Frances Wood, *No dogs and not many Chinese: Treaty port life in China, 1843–1943*, London: John Murray, 1998, pp. 2–3 and 297.

29   Richard P. Dobson, *China cycle*, London: Macmillan, 1946, p. 13.

30   Banque de France, 'Offshoring', *Banque de France Bulletin Digest*, no. 133, 2005, pp. 21–35; Norman D. Hanwell, 'France takes inventory in China', *Far Eastern Survey*, 7, no. 19 (Sept. 1938), pp. 217–25.

31   Shannon R. Brown, 'Cakes and oil: Technology transfer and Chinese soybean processing, 1860–1895', *Comparative Studies in Society and History*, 23, no. 3 (July 1981), pp. 449–63.

32   Feuerwerker, *The foreign establishment*, p. 92.

33   Ibid., pp. 61–2.

34   Ibid., pp. 68–77.

35   Ibid., pp. 106–7.

36   Guy Brossollet, *Les Français de Shanghai, 1849–1949*, Paris: Belin, 1999, pp. 227–32.

37   Arthur Ransome, *The Chinese puzzle*, London: Allen and Unwin, 1927; Robert Bickers, *Britain in China: Community, culture and colonialism 1900–1949*, Manchester University Press, 1999.

38   Foremost among these historians is Wood, *Treaty port life in China, 1843–1943*; see also Nicholas R. Clifford, *Spoilt children of empire: Westerners in Shanghai and the Chinese revolution of the 1920s*, Hanover, NH: University Press of New England, 1991, p. 76.

39   Robert N. Tharp, *They called us White Chinese: The story of a lifetime of service to God and mankind*, Charlotte, NC: Eva E. Tharp Publications, 1994.

40   John K. Fairbank, *Chinabound: A fifty-year memoir*, New York: Harper and Row, 1982, p. 51.

41   Feuerwerker, *The foreign establishment*, p. 104; see also Thomas Lawton, *A time of transition: Two collectors of Chinese art*, Lawrence, KS: Spencer Museum of Art, 1991, pp. 65–97.

42   Carl Crow, *Four hundred million customers*, New York: Halcyon House, 1937, p. 17.

43   Ida Pruitt, *A China childhood*, San Francisco: Chinese Materials Center, 1978.

44   Pearl Buck, *My several worlds, a personal record*, New York: John Day, 1954, p. 10.

45   Innes Jackson, *China only yesterday*, London: Faber and Faber, 1938;

Reginald F. Johnston, *Twilight in the forbidden city*, Hong Kong: Oxford University Press, 1985.

46  Rudolph Löwenthal, *The religious periodical press in China*, Beijing: Synodal Commission in China, 1940, pp. 252–3 and 269.

47  Constantin Rissov, *Le dragon enchaîné: De Chiang Kai-shek à Mao Ze-dong, trente-cinq ans d'intimité avec la Chine*, Paris: Robert Laffont, 1985.

48  John Haffenden, *William Empson: Among the mandarins*, Oxford University Press, 2005.

49  For instance Zhang Kaiyuan, 'Chinese perspective: A brief review of the historical research on Christianity in China', in Stephen Uhalley and Xiaoxin Wu (eds.), *China and Christianity: Burdened past, hopeful future*, Armonk, NY: M. E. Sharpe, 2001, pp. 29–42.

50  Tharp, *They called us White Chinese*.

51  James C. Thomson, *While China faced West: American reformers in Nationalist China, 1928–1937*, Cambridge, MA: Harvard University Press, 1969, pp. 76–9.

52  Feuerwerker, *The foreign establishment*, pp. 39–49.

53  Thomson, *While China faced West*, pp. 35–8.

54  A. J. Nathan, *A history of the China International Famine Relief Commission*, Cambridge, MA: Harvard University Press, 1965; see also Gerald Yorke, *China changes*, London: Jonathan Cape, 1935, pp. 70–1.

55  Thomas Rawski, *Economic growth in prewar China*, Berkeley: University of California Press, 1989, pp. 235–6.

56  This point was made by Jonathan Mirksy in a review of a biography of Edgar Snow in *The New York Review of Books* in February 1989, only to be atttacked by John K. Fairbank, doyen of Chinese studies at Harvard; see 'Mao and Snow', *The New York Review of Books*, 36, no. 7, 27 April 1989.

57  Wood, *No dogs and not many Chinese*, p. 301.

## Chapter 4

1  William C. Kirby, 'The internationalization of China: Foreign relations at home and abroad', *China Quarterly*, no. 150 (June 1997), pp. 437–8.

2  Tang Qihua, 'Qingmo minchu Zhongguo dui "Haiya baohe hui" zhi canyu (1899–1917)' (China's participation in the Hague Peace Conferences, 1899–1917), *Guoli zhengzhi daxue lishi xuebao*, no. 23 (May 2005), pp. 45–90; see also Xu Guoqi, *China and the Great War: China's pursuit of a new national identity and internationalization*, Cambridge University Press, 2005.

3  Pao-Chin Chu, *V. K. Wellington Koo: A case study of China's diplomat and diplomacy of nationalism, 1912–1966*, Hong Kong: Chinese University

Press, 1981; Stephen G. Craft, *V. K. Wellington Koo and the emergence of modern China*, Lexington: University Press of Kentucky, 2004.

4    F. T. Cheng, *East and West: Episodes in a sixty years' journey*, London: Hutchinson, 1951.

5    Kirby, 'The internationalization of China', pp. 448 and 455.

6    'International Convention for the Suppression of the Traffic in Women and Children', *American Journal of International Law*, 18, no. 3 (July 1924), pp. 130–7.

7    Manley O. Hudson, 'The registration of treaties', *American Journal of International Law*, 24, no. 4 (Oct. 1930), pp. 754–5; see also L. K. Quan, *China's relations with the League of Nations, 1919–1936*, Hong Kong: Asiatic Press, 1939; of interest is also Jürgen Osterhammel, '"Technical co-operation" between the League of Nations and China', *Modern Asian Studies*, 13, no. 4 (1979), pp. 661–80.

8    See International Anti-Opium Association, *The war against opium*, Tianjin: Tientsin Press, 1922, pp. 22–4; William McAllister, *Drug diplomacy in the twentieth century: An international history*, London: Routledge, 2000, pp. 24–7; Zhou Yongming, *Anti-drug crusades in twentieth-century China: Nationalism, history, and state-building*, Lanham, MD: Rowman and Littlefield, 1999, pp. 27–32.

9    Frank Dikötter, *Crime, punishment and the prison in modern China*, New York: Columbia University Press, 2002, pp. 39, 50, 65, 114–5, 142–3, 200, 227 and 345–6.

10   Frank Dikötter, *Imperfect conceptions: Medical knowledge, birth defects and eugenics in China*, New York: Columbia University Press, 1998, Chapter 2.

11   Zheng Shengtian, 'Waves lashed the Bund from the West: Shanghai's art scene in the 1930s' in Jo-Anne Birnie Danzker, Ken Lum and Zheng Shengtian (eds.), *Shanghai modern, 1919–1945*, Ostfildern-Ruit: Hatje Cantz, 2004, pp. 174–99.

12   Beijing tushuguan (ed.) *Minguo shiqi zong shumu, 1911–1949* (Catalogue of books published in the republican era, 1911–1949), Beijing: Shumu wenxian chubanshe: Xinhua shudian, 1986–96.

13   See Dikötter, *Crime, punishment and the prison in modern China*, the bibliography in particular; as a specific example, twelve out of these twenty-five books carry the title *Penology*, although at least thirty books with that title are known to have been published in the republican era; see the more complete catalogue complied by Zhongguo zhengfa daxue tushuguan (ed.), *Zhongguo falü tushu zongmu* (Catalogue of law books in Chinese), Beijing: Zhongguo zhengfa daxue chubanshe, 1991, pp. 486–92.

14   Quanguo diyi zhongxin tushuguan weiyuanhui quanguo tushu lianhe mulu bianji zu (ed.), *Quanguo zhongwen qikan lianhe mulu, 1833–1949*

(Catalogue of periodicals in Chinese, 1833–1949), Beijing: Beijing tushuguan, 1961.

15 Otto Struve, 'The decline of international cooperation in astronomy', *Science*, 87, no. 2260 (April 1938), pp. 364–5.

16 See Dikötter, *Crime, punishment and the prison in modern China*, Chapters 4 and 5, in particular pp. 199–202.

17 Ibid., pp. 394–5.

18 Maurice Freedman, 'Sociology in and of China', *British Journal of Sociology*, 13, no. 2 (June 1962), p. 113.

19 Leonard Shih-lien Hsu, 'The sociological movement in China', *Pacific Affairs*, 4, no. 4 (April 1931), pp. 283–307.

20 Bingham Dai, *Opium addiction in Chicago*, orig. 1937, Montclair, NJ: Patterson Smith, 1970; he was most recently recognised as a pioneer in the *Newsletter of the Society for Applied Anthropology*, 13, no. 1 (Feb. 2002), p. 3; see also Geoffrey Blowers, 'Bingham Dai, Adolf Storfer, and the tentative beginnings of psychoanalytic culture in China: 1935–1941', *Psychoanalysis and History*, 6, no. 1 (2004), pp. 93–105.

21 Julean Arnold, *China through the American window*, Shanghai: American Chamber of Commerce, 1932, p. 33.

22 See E-tu Zen Sun, 'The growth of the academic community, 1912–1949', in John K. Fairbank and Albert Feuerwerker (eds.), *The Cambridge history of China*, vol. 13, part 2, p. 364; C. P. Fitzgerald, 'Review of *Chinese Intellectuals and the West* by Y. C. Wang', *Pacific Affairs*, 40, no. 1 (Spring 1967), p. 140; Jerome Ch'en has written some magnificent pages on the returned students; see his *China and the West: Society and culture, 1815–1937*, London: Hutchinson, 1979, pp. 151–202.

23 Jing Cheng Qu, 'Chinese physicists educated in Germany and America: Their scientific contributions and their impact on China's higher education (1900–1949)', doctoral dissertation, Ohio State University, 1998.

24 Rudolph Löwenthal, *The religious periodical press in China*, Beijing: Synodal Commission in China, 1940, p. 291.

25 Olga Lang, *Chinese family and society*, New Haven: Yale University Press, 1946, p. 89.

26 A. S. Roe, *Chance and change in China*, London: Heinemann, 1920, p. 27.

27 G. L. Dickinson, *Appearances: Being notes of travel*, London: Dent, 1914, p. 68.

28 Sidney D. Gamble, *North China villages: Social, political, and economic activities before 1933*, Berkeley: University of California Press, 1963, pp. 104–8.

29 D. H. Kulp, *Country life in south China: The sociology of familism*, Taipei: Ch'eng-wen, 1966, pp. 226–33.

30 Elizabeth VanderVen, 'Village-state cooperation: Modern community schools and their funding, Haicheng County, Fengtian, 1905–1931', *Modern China*, 31, no. 2 (April 2005), pp. 204–35.

31 Frank Dikötter, *The discourse of race in modern China*, Stanford University Press, 1992; both quotations appear on p. 163.

32 Jerome Ch'en, *China and the West: Society and culture, 1815–1937*, London: Hutchinson, 1979, pp. 108–11.

33 Lian Xi, *The conversion of missionaries: Liberalism in American Protestant missions in China, 1907–1932*, Pennsylvania Park: Pennsylvania State University Press, 1997, p. 158.

34 Kenneth Scott Latourette, *A history of the expansion of Christianity*, New York: Harper, 1945, vol. 7, pp. 335 and 369.

35 Ibid., vol. 7, p. 342.

36 Ibid., vol. 7, pp. 352–3.

37 John K. Fairbank, 'The place of Protestant writings in China's cultural history', in Suzanne Wilson Barnett and John K. Fairbank (eds.), *Christianity in China: Early Protestant missionary writings*, Cambridge, MA: Harvard University Press, 1984, pp. 7–13; see also Kathleen L. Lodwick, *Crusaders against opium: Protestant missionaries in China, 1874–1917*, Lexington: University Press of Kentucky, 1995, pp. 53 and 66–67.

38 See Norman Howard Cliff, 'The life and theology of Watchman Nee, including a study of the Little Flock Movement which he founded', London: Open University, 1983, MPhil dissertation, pp. 62–77.

39 See Bob Whyte, *Unfinished encounter: China and Christianity*, London: Collins, 1988; on the True Jesus Church, see Allen J. Swanson and Grace Lo, *The Church in Taiwan: Profile 1980, a review of the past, a projection for the future*, Pasadena: William Carey Library, 1981, pp. 76–9; see also Daniel H. Bays, 'Indigenous Protestant churches in China', in Steven Kaplan (ed.), *Indigenous responses to Western Christianity*, New York University Press, 1995, pp. 124–43.

40 Cliff, 'The life and theology of Watchman Nee', pp. 31–44.

41 These numbers were furnished as early as in 1945 in Latourette, *A history of the expansion of Christianity*, vol. 7, p. 370.

42 Gabriele Goldfuss, 'Binding sutras and modernity: The life and times of the Chinese layman Yang Wenhui (1837–1911)', *Studies in Central and East Asian Religion*, vol. 9 (1996).

43 Darui Long, 'An interfaith dialogue between the Chinese Buddhist leader Taixu and Christians', *Buddhist-Christian Studies*, vol. 20 (2000), pp. 167–89.

44 Francesca Tarocco, 'Attuning the Dharma: The cultural practices of modern Chinese Buddhists', doctoral dissertation, University of London, 2004.

45  Holmes Welch, *The Buddhist revival in China*, Cambridge, MA: Harvard University Press, 1968.

46  Emma Louise Benignus, 'Current religious trends in China', *Journal of Bible and Religion*, 15, no. 4 (Oct. 1947), pp. 199–205.

47  Welch, *The Buddhist revival in China*, pp. 98 and 262; his examples, however, all date from the 1920s, and for later periods one could add Yorke, *China changes*, p. 174, who mentions construction activity all over central China in the mid-1930s, although he was still berated in a review by G. E. Taylor for not having sufficiently emphasised the amount of building performed by lay practitioners rather than by professional monks, a critical point which might be extended to Welch's work as well; see G. E. Taylor, 'Review', *Pacific Affairs*, 9, no. 3 (Sept. 1936), pp. 464–6.

48  See the pioneering work of a member of the Department of Journalism at Yenching University, Rudolph Löwenthal, *The religious periodical press in China*, Beijing: Synodal Commission in China, 1940, pp. 211–50.

49  Dru C. Gladney, 'Sino-Middle Eastern perspectives and relations since the Gulf War: Views from below', *International Journal of Middle East Studies*, 26, no. 4 (Nov. 1994), p. 679.

50  Derk Bodde, 'China's Muslim minority', *Far Eastern Survey*, 15, no. 18 (Sept. 1946), pp. 281–4; Chan Wing-tsit, *Religious trends in modern China*, New York: Octagon Books, 1969, pp. 186–216; see also Andrew D.W. Forbes, *Warlords and Muslims in Chinese Central Asia: A political history of republican Sinkiang, 1911–1949*, Cambridge University Press, 1986, and Linda Benson, *The Ili Rebellion: The Moslem challenge to Chinese authority in Xinjiang, 1944–1949*, Armonk, NY: M. E. Sharpe, 1990.

51  Dru C. Gladney, 'Islam', *Journal of Asian Studies*, 54, no. 2 (May 1995), pp. 371–8.

52  Darui Long, 'An interfaith dialogue between the Chinese Buddhist leader Taixu and Christians', *Buddhist-Christian Studies*, vol. 20 (2000), pp. 167–89.

53  Ibid., p. 179; Chan, *Religious trends in modern China*, pp. 82–3.

54  Dikötter, *Crime, punishment and the prison in modern China*, pp. 109–10.

55  Don A. Pittman, 'The modern Buddhist reformer T'ai-hsü on Christianity', *Buddhist-Christian Studies*, vol. 13 (1993), pp. 79–80.

56  Lewis Hodous, 'The Chinese Church of the Five Religions', *Journal of Religion*, 4, no. 1 (Jan. 1924), pp. 71–6; Paul de Witt Twinem, 'Modern syncretic religious societies in China', *Journal of Religion*, 5, no. 5 (Sept. 1925), pp. 463–82.

57  Eileen Chang, *Written on water*, translated by Andrew F. Jones, New York: Columbia University Press, 2005.

58  Jo-Anne Birnie Danzker, 'Shanghai modern', in Jo-Anne Birnie Danzker,

Ken Lum and Zheng Shengtian (eds.), *Shanghai modern, 1919–1945*, Ostfildern-Ruit: Hatje Cantz, 2004, p. 64.

59   Shelagh Vainker, 'Modern Chinese painting in London, 1935', in Danzker, Lum and Zheng, *Shanghai modern, 1919–1945*, pp. 118–23.

60   Zhang Zhen, *An amorous history of the silver screen: Shanghai cinema, 1896–1937*, University of Chicago Press, 2005, pp. 288–96.

61   Ibid., p. 240.

62   Ibid., p. 199; this line also appears in Jay Leyda, *Dianying: An account of films and the film audience in China*, Cambridge, MA: M.I.T. Press, 1972, p. 62, who quotes Cheng Jihua, *Zhongguo dianying fazhan shi* (History of the development of Chinese cinema), Beijing: Zhongguo dianying chubanshe, 1963, vol. 1, p. 133.

63   Fu Poshek, *Between Shanghai and Hong Kong: The politics of Chinese cinemas*, Stanford University Press, 2003, pp. xiv and 55–63.

64   The exception is Edwin Kin-keung Lai, 'The life and art photography of Lang Jingshan (1892–1995)', doctoral dissertation, University of Hong Kong, 2000.

65   'Chinese show breaks nude taboo', BBC News, 29 Jan. 2001.

66   Heinz von Perckhammer, *Edle Nacktheit in China* (The culture of the nude in China), Berlin: Eigenbrödler, 1928.

67   See Frank Dikötter, *Exotic commodities: Modern objects and everyday life in China*, New York: Columbia University Press, 2007, Chapter 10.

68   For an introduction, see Editions Revue Noire (eds.), *Anthology of African and Indian Ocean Photography*, Paris: Editions Revue Noire, 1999.

69   Chao Mei-pa, 'The trend of modern Chinese music', *T'ien Hsia Monthly*, no. 4 (March 1937), pp. 269–86; *L'Artiste Chinois Chao Mei-Pa. Appréciations*, Brussels: Wellens and Godenne, n.d. (1933?); see also Sheila Melvin and Jindong Cai, *Rhapsody in red: How Western classical music became Chinese*, New York: Algora Publishing, 2004.

70   Alexander Tcherepnine, 'Music in modern China', *The Musical Quarterly*, 21, no. 4 (Oct. 1935), pp. 391–400.

71   Andrew F. Jones, *Yellow music: Media culture and colonial modernity in the Chinese Jazz Age*, Durham: Duke University Press, 2001.

72   Jonathan Stock, 'Reconsidering the past: Zhou Xuan and the rehabilitation of early twentieth-century popular music', *Asian Music*, 26, no. 2 (Spring 1995), pp. 119–35; Andreas Steen, 'Zhou Xuan: When will the gentleman come back again?', *Chime*, nos. 14–15 (1999–2000), pp. 125–53; Sue Tuohy, 'Metropolitan sounds: Music in Chinese films of the 1930s' in Zhang Yingjin (ed.), *Cinema and urban culture in Shanghai, 1922–1943*, Stanford University Press, 1999, pp. 200–21.

73   Jones, *Yellow music*, p. 15.

# Chapter 5

1 John K. Fairbank, Edwin O. Reischauer and Albert M. Craig, *East Asia: Tradition and transformation*, Boston: Houghton Mifflin, 1973, p. 178.

2 Frank Dikötter, *Exotic commodities: Modern objects and everyday life in China*, New York: Columbia University Press, 2007.

3 David Faure, *China and capitalism: A history of business enterprise in modern China*, Hong Kong University Press, 2006, pp. 45–64; not all enterprises immediately took advantage of the Company Law; see William C. Kirby, 'China unincorporated: Company law and business enterprise in twentieth-century China', *Journal of Asian Studies*, 54, No. 1 (Feb. 1995), pp. 43–6.

4 'International Convention Relating to the Simplification of Customs Formalities', *American Journal of International Law*, 19, no. 4, Supplement: Official Documents (Oct. 1925), pp. 146–66.

5 Hao Yen-p'ing, *The commercial revolution in nineteenth-century China: The rise of Sino-Western mercantile capitalism*, Berkeley: University of California Press, 1986; Philip Richardson, *Economic change in China, c. 1800–1950*, Cambridge University Press, 1999, p. 42.

6 Richardson, *Economic change in China, c. 1800–1950*, p. 43.

7 Ibid., pp. 43–4.

8 Thomas Rawski, *Economic growth in prewar China*, Berkeley: University of California Press, 1989, pp. 5–7.

9 Ibid., pp. 6–8.

10 Jack Gray, *Rebellions and revolutions: China from the 1800s to the 1980s*, Oxford University Press, 1990, p. 168.

11 Richard A. Kraus, *Cotton and cotton goods in China, 1918–1936*, New York: Garland, 1980, p. 2; Philip C. C. Huang, *The peasant family and rural development in the Yangzi delta, 1350–1988*, Stanford University Press, 1990, pp. 98, 116 and 152.

12 *Trade reports*, 'Report on the trade of China, 1936', 1936.

13 Gray, *Rebellions and revolutions*, pp. 152–3.

14 Chinese Ministry of Information, *China handbook, 1937–1945: A comprehensive survey of major developments in China in eight years of war*, New York: Da Capo Press, 1947, pp. 404–5; see also G. C. Allen and A. G. Donnithorne, *Western enterprise in Far Eastern economic development: China and Japan*, New York: Macmillan, 1954, p. 119.

15 James Hsioung Lee, *A half century of memories*, Hong Kong: South China Photo-Process Printing Co., n.d., 1960s, p. 89.

16 Ibid., p. 85.

17 Gray, *Rebellions and revolutions*, p. 156.

18   John L. Buck, *Land utilization in China*, Nanjing: University of Nanking, 1937; Gray, *Rebellions and revolutions*, p. 160.

19   Gray, *Rebellions and revolutions*, pp. 160–1.

20   Loren Brandt, *Commercialization and agricultural development: Central and eastern China, 1870–1937*, Cambridge University Press, 1989.

21   Gray, *Rebellions and revolutions*, p. 163.

22   This is not the place to review these debates, but the interested reader can find an excellent overview in Richardson, *Economic change in China, c. 1800–1950*.

23   Stephen L. Morgan, 'Economic growth and the biological standard of living in China, 1880–1930', *Economics and human biology*, no. 2 (2004), pp. 197–218.

24   David Faure, *The rural economy of pre-liberation China: Trade expansion and peasant livelihood in Jiangsu and Guangdong, 1870 to 1937*, Hong Kong: Oxford University Press, 1989, p. 203; see also Brandt, *Commercialization and agricultural development*.

25   Huang, *The peasant family and rural development in the Yangzi delta, 1350–1988*, p. 15.

26   Dikötter, *Exotic commodities*, Chapter 2.

27   Wenshi ziliao yanjiu weiyuanhui (ed.), *Xinhai geming huiyi lu* (Reminiscences about the revolution of 1911), Beijing: Wenshi ziliao chubanshe, 1981, p. 366.

28   M. B. Treudley, *The men and women of Chung Ho Ch'ang*, Taipei: Orient Cultural Service, 1971, p. 40.

29   'Swatow', *Decennial reports, 1922–31*, Shanghai: Statistical Department of the Inspectorate General of Customs, 1933, p. 162.

30   Brian H. Low, 'The standard of living', in John L. Buck, *Land utilization in China*, Nanjing: University of Nanking, 1937, p. 459.

31   Liu Shanlin, *Xiyang feng: Xiyang faming zai Zhongguo* (Inventions from the West in China), Shanghai: Shanghai guji chubanshe, 1999, p. 142.

32   Zhu Zhihong, *Baxianzhi* (A history of Ba county), orig. 1939, Chengdu: Bashu shushe, 1992, vol. 13, p. 4.

33   Stephen Mennell, *All manners of food: Eating and taste in England and France from the Middle Ages to the present*, London: Blackwell, 1985, pp. 321 and 329.

34   Dikötter, *Exotic commodities*, Chapter 9.

35   Andrew Nathan, 'A constitutional republic: The Peking government, 1916–28', in Denis Twitchett and John K. Fairbank (eds.), *The Cambridge history of China*, vol. 12, part 1, Cambridge University Press, 1983, pp. 267 and 272–3.

36   Department of Overseas Trade, *Economic conditions in China to September 1st, 1929*, London: Stationery Office, 1930, p. 26.

37 W. G. Sewell, *The land and life of China*, London: Edinburgh House Press, 1945, pp. 13–4.

38 Victor Purcell, *Chinese evergreen*, London: Michael Joseph, 1938, pp. 152, 173–4, 191, 244.

39 Gerald Yorke, *China changes*, London: Jonathan Cape, 1935, p. 89.

40 L. H. Dudley Buxton, *China: The land and the people*, Oxford: Clarendon Press, 1929, p. 139.

41 Peter Fleming, *One's company: A journey to China*, London: Jonathan Cape, 1934, p. 200.

42 'Report on the trade of Amoy, for the year 1883', *Report on the trade at the ports of China for the year 1883*, Shanghai: Imperial Maritime Customs' Press, 1884, p. 294.

43 Gong Debo, *Gong Debo huiyi lu* (Reminiscences of Gong Debo), Taipei: Longwen chubanshe, 1989, p. 11.

44 Lena E. Johnston, *China and her peoples*, London: Church Missionary Society, 1925, p. 118.

45 Hiroyuki Hokari, 'Donghua yiyuan yu huaren wangluo' (The Tung-Wah Hospital and Chinese networks) in South China Research Center and South China Research Circle (eds.), *Jingying wenhua: Zhongguo shehui danyuan de guanli yu yunzuo* (Managing culture: Chinese organizations in action), Hong Kong Educational Publishing Co., 1999, pp. 229–43.

46 Department of Overseas Trade, *Economic conditions in China to September 1st, 1929*, pp. 22–3.

47 Wang Fuming, 'Making a living: Agriculture, industry and commerce in eastern Hebei, 1870–1937', doctoral dissertation, Iowa State University, 1998, p. 154; see also Ernest P. Liang, *China: Railways and agricultural development, 1875–1935*, University of Chicago Press, 1982.

48 Chang Jui-te, 'Technology tranfer in modern China: The case of railway enterprise (1876–1937)', *Modern Asian Studies*, 27, no. 2 (1993), p. 291.

49 Lee, *A half century of memories*, p. 22.

50 Department of Overseas Trade, *Economic conditions in China to September 1st, 1929*, p. 30.

51 Harrison Forman, *Changing China*, New York: Crown, 1948, pp. 278–9.

52 Dikötter, *Exotic commodities*, Chapter 4.

## Chapter 6

1 Jeffrey Brooks, 'Official xenophobia and popular cosmopolitanism in early Soviet Russia', *American Historical Review*, 97, no. 5 (Dec. 1992), pp. 1431–48.

2   Valerie Hansen, *The open empire: A history of China to 1600*, New York: W. W. Norton, 2000.

3   Joanna Waley-Cohen, *The sextants of Beijing: Global currents in Chinese history*, New York: W. W. Norton, 1999.

# A Note on Further Reading for the Non-Chinese Reader

Historians build monuments, and the best way to stay grounded and view these paper edifices from a critical distance is full immersion in primary sources. There are numerous and often very helpful sources on republican China available in English to the non-specialist reader, including sociological surveys, trade reports, travel literature and memoirs. A few used in this study are Olga Lang, *Chinese Family and Society*, New Haven: Yale University Press, 1946; M. B. Treudley, *The Men and Women of Chung Ho Ch'ang*, Taipei: Orient Cultural Service, 1971; John L. Buck, *Land Utilization in China*, Nanjing: University of Nanking, 1937; Sidney D. Gamble, *North China Villages: Social, Political, and Economic Activities before 1933*, Berkeley: University of California Press, 1963; Gerald Yorke, *China Changes*, London: Jonathan Cape, 1935; Rudolph Löwenthal, *The Religious Periodical Press in China*, Beijing: Synodal Commission in China, 1940. Given the cosmopolitan nature of republican China, there are also many excellent sources in English written by Chinese individuals, two examples used in this book being F. T. Cheng, *East and West: Episodes in a Sixty Years' Journey*, London: Hutchinson, 1951 and James Hsioung Lee, *A Half-Century of Memories*, Hong Kong: South China Photo-Process Printing Co., n.d., 1960s.

In order to contextualise these primary sources, the non-specialist may wish to consult a general history of modern China, and I recommend Jack Gray, *Rebellions and Revolutions: China from the 1800s to the 1980s*, Oxford University Press, 1990, which is provocative yet systematic on the period up to 1949. More specifically on the cosmopolitan aspects of modern China, Jerome Ch'en, *China and the West: Society and Culture, 1815–1937*, London: Hutchinson, 1979, has aged gracefully thanks to firm anchoring in primary material and will repay close reading. Two articles are closely related to some of the themes explored in this book and deserve special mention, namely William C. Kirby, 'The internationalization of China: Foreign relations at home and abroad', *China Quarterly*, no. 150 (June 1997), pp. 433–58 and Philip C. C. Huang, 'Biculturality in modern China and in Chinese studies', *Modern China*, 26, no. 1 (Jan. 2000), pp. 3–31; pioneering was Ramon H. Myers and Thomas A. Metzger, 'Sinological shadows: The state of modern China studies in the United States', *Australian Journal of Chinese Affairs*, no. 4 (July 1980), pp. 1–34.

It is not the intention here to list an exhaustive bibliography on the many topics broached in this book, but merely to provide the reader with an introduction to the more critical literature in the field, which implies that many of the usual suspects do not get a mention (although any recent textbook on the history of modern China, for instance Jonathan D. Spence, *The Search for Modern China*, New York: W. W. Norton, 1999, second edition, will provide a general bibliography). Essential on the 'warlords' is the work of Arthur Waldron, 'The warlord: Twentieth-century Chinese understandings of violence, militarism, and imperialism', *The American Historical Review*, 96, no. 4 (Oct. 1991), pp. 1073–100, Arthur Waldron, 'Warlordism versus federalism: The revival of a debate?', *The China Quarterly*, no. 121 (March 1990), pp. 116–28, and Arthur Waldron, *From War to Nationalism: China's Turning Point, 1924–1925*, Cambridge University Press, 1995, while useful insights on federalism are offered in Jean Chesneaux, 'The federalist movement in China, 1920–1923' in Jack Gray (ed.), *Modern China's Search for a Political Form*, Oxford University Press, 1969 and Leslie H. Dingyan Chen, *Chen Jiongming and the Federalist Movement: Regional Leadership and Nation Building in Early Republican China*, Ann Arbor: University of Michigan Press, 1999. Particularly helpful is R. Keith Schoppa, 'Province and nation: The Chekiang Provincial Autonomy Movement, 1917–1927', *Journal of Asian Studies*, 36, no. 4 (Aug. 1977), pp. 661–74. Besides the Ministry of Justice, analysed in Frank Dikötter, *Crime, Punishment and the Prison in Modern China*, New York: Columbia University Press, 2002, there is no other detailed study of any one government institution throughout the first half of the twentieth century, although a number of ministries are presented in Julia C. Strauss, *Strong Institutions in Weak Polities: State Building in Republican China, 1927–1940*, Oxford University Press, 1998. On elections and democracy from 1902 to 1949 see Roger R. Thompson, 'The lessons of defeat: Transforming the Qing state after the Boxer War', *Modern Asian Studies*, 37, no. 4 (Oct. 2003), pp 769–73; Mark Elvin, 'The gentry democracy in Chinese Shanghai, 1905–1914' in Jack Gray (ed.), *Modern China's Search for a Political Form*, Oxford University Press, 1969, pp. 41–66; John H. Fincher, *Chinese Democracy: The Self-Government Movement in Local, Provincial and National Politics, 1905–1914*, London: Croom Helm, 1981; Andrew J. Nathan, *Chinese Democracy*, New York: Knopf, 1985; Marina Svensson, *Debating Human Rights in China: A Conceptual and Political History*, Lanham: Rowman and Littlefield, 2002; Roger R. Thompson, *China's Local Councils in the Age of Constitutional Reform, 1898–1911*, Cambridge, MA: Harvard University Press, 1995; and on oppositional politics one should read Roger B. Jeans (ed.), *Roads Not Taken: The Struggle of Opposition Parties in Twentieth-Century China*, Boulder: Westview Press, 1992; Eugene Lubot, *Liberalism in an Illiberal Age: New Culture Liberals in Republican China, 1919–1937*, Westport, CN: Greenwood Press, 1982; Louise Edwards, *Gender, Politics and Democracy: Women's Suffrage in China*, Stanford University Press, 2008; Edmund S. K. Fung, *In Search of Chinese Democracy: Civil Opposition in Nationalist China, 1929–1949*, Cambridge University Press, 2000; and William C. Kirby (ed.), *Realms of Freedom in Modern China*, Stanford University Press, 2004. On local activism see Mary B. Rankin, *Elite Activism and Political Transformation in China, Zhejiang Province, 1865–1911*, Stanford University Press, 1986; William T. Rowe, *Hankow: Conflict and Community in a Chinese City*, Stanford University Press, 1989; David Strand, *Rickshaw Beijing: City People and Politics in the 1920s*, Berkeley: University of California Press, 1989; Robert J. Culp, 'Elite association and local politics in republican China: Educational institutions in Jiashan and Lanqi Counties, Zhejiang, 1911–1937', *Modern China*, 20, no. 4 (Oct. 1994), pp. 446–77; and the overview by Mary B. Rankin, 'State and society in early republican politics, 1912–18', *China Quarterly*, no. 150 (June 1997), pp. 260–81.

On overseas Chinese, an elegant introduction is offered by Wang

Gungwu, *The Chinese Overseas: From Earthbound China to the Quest for Autonomy*, Cambridge, MA: Harvard University Press, 2000; see also the superb essay by Mark Ravinder Frost, 'Transcultural diaspora: The Straits Chinese in Singapore, 1819–1918', Working Paper Series no. 10, Asia Research Institute, National University of Singapore, 2003. Ng Lun Ngai-Ha, 'The role of Hong Kong educated Chinese in the shaping of modern China', *Modern Asian Studies*, 17, no. 1 (1983), pp. 137–63; John M. Carroll, *Edge of Empires: Chinese Elites and British Colonials in Hong Kong*, Cambridge, MA: Harvard University Press, 2005; and Kingsley Bolton, *Chinese Englishes: A Sociolinguistic History*, Cambridge University Press, 2003, are all highly original. On foreigners, essential are James C. Thomson, *While China Faced West: American Reformers in Nationalist China, 1928–1937*, Cambridge, MA: Harvard University Press, 1969; Albert Feuerwerker, *The Foreign Establishment in China in the Early Twentieth Century*, Ann Arbor: University of Michigan Press, 1976; Nicholas R. Clifford, *Spoilt Children of Empire: Westerners in Shanghai and the Chinese Revolution of the 1920s*, Hanover, NH: University Press of New England, 1991; Frances Wood, *No Dogs and Not Many Chinese: Treaty Port Life in China, 1843–1943*, London: John Murray, 1998; and Guy Brossollet, *Les Français de Shanghai, 1849–1949*, Paris: Belin, 1999.

Diplomacy is understudied, but a superb essay is William C. Kirby, 'The internationalization of China: Foreign relations at home and abroad', *China Quarterly*, no. 150 (June 1997), pp. 433–58; see also Pao-Chin Chu, *V. K. Wellington Koo: A Case Study of China's Diplomat and Diplomacy of Nationalism, 1912–1966*, Hong Kong: Chinese University Press, 1981; Stephen G. Craft, *V. K. Wellington Koo and the Emergence of Modern China*, Lexington: University Press of Kentucky, 2004; and Xu Guoqi, *China and the Great War: China's Pursuit of a New National Identity and Internationalization*, Cambridge University Press, 2005. On returned students and the academic community one should start with E-tu Zen Sun, 'The growth of the academic community, 1912–1949' in John K. Fairbank and Albert Feuerwerker (eds.), *The Cambridge History of China*, vol. 13, part 2, pp. 361–420; Jerome Ch'en has written some magnificent pages on the returned students in his *China and the West: Society and Culture, 1815–1937*, London:

Hutchinson, 1979. On schools, see the pioneering work of Elizabeth VanderVen, 'Village-state cooperation: Modern community schools and their funding, Haicheng County, Fengtian, 1905–1931', *Modern China*, 31, no. 2 (April 2005), pp. 204–35. Religion can be explored through the work of Kenneth Scott Latourette, *A History of the Expansion of Christianity*, New York: Harper, 1945; Holmes Welch, *The Buddhist Revival in China*, Cambridge, MA: Harvard University Press, 1968; Chan Wing-tsit, *Religious Trends in Modern China*, New York: Octagon Books, 1969; Norman Howard Cliff, 'The life and theology of Watchman Nee, including a study of the Little Flock Movement which he founded', MPhil dissertation, London: Open University, 1983; Daniel H. Bays, 'Indigenous Protestant churches in China' in Steven Kaplan (ed.), *Indigenous Responses to Western Christianity*, New York University Press, 1995, pp. 124–43; and Francesca Tarocco, 'Attuning the Dharma: The cultural practices of modern Chinese Buddhists', doctoral dissertation, University of London, 2004. For a general introduction to art in republican China, albeit limited to Shanghai, see Jo-Anne Birnie Danzker, Ken Lum and Zheng Shengtian (eds.), *Shanghai Modern, 1919–1945*, Ostfildern-Ruit: Hatje Cantz, 2004. On cinema one will benefit from Fu Poshek, *Between Shanghai and Hong Kong: The Politics of Chinese Cinemas*, Stanford University Press, 2003 and Zhang Zhen, *An Amorous History of the Silver Screen: Shanghai Cinema, 1896–1937*, University of Chicago Press, 2005, while popular music is approached by Jonathan Stock, 'Reconsidering the past: Zhou Xuan and the rehabilitation of early twentieth-century popular music', *Asian Music*, 26, no. 2 (Spring 1995), pp. 119–35, and Andrew F. Jones, *Yellow Music: Media Culture and Colonial Modernity in the Chinese Jazz Age*, Durham: Duke University Press, 2001; on classical music see Sheila Melvin and Jindong Cai, *Rhapsody in Red: How Western Classical Music Became Chinese*, New York: Algora Publishing, 2004. On China's preeminent photographer consult Edwin Kin-keung Lai, 'The life and art photography of Lang Jingshan (1892–1995)', doctoral dissertation, University of Hong Kong, 2000, and on vernacular photography see Frank Dikötter, *Exotic Commodities: Modern Objects and Everyday Life in China*, New York: Columbia University Press, 2006, Chapter 10.

The best introduction to the complex literature on economic history is Philip Richardson, *Economic Change in China, c. 1800–1950,* Cambridge University Press, 1999. Other superb contributions include Yen-p'ing Hao, *The Commercial Revolution in Nineteenth-Century China: The Rise of Sino-Western Mercantile Capitalism,* Berkeley: University of California Press, 1986; Loren Brandt, *Commercialization and Agricultural Development: Central and Eastern China, 1870–1937,* Cambridge University Press, 1989; David Faure, *The Rural Economy of Pre-liberation China: Trade Expansion and Peasant Livelihood in Jiangsu and Guangdong, 1870 to 1937,* Hong Kong: Oxford University Press, 1989; Thomas Rawski, *Economic Growth in Prewar China,* Berkeley: University of California Press, 1989; David Faure, *China and Capitalism: A History of Business Enterprise in Modern China,* Hong Kong University Press, 2006. As these titles show, there is a considerable body of work on the quantitative changes in the republican economy, although research on qualitative aspects remains sparse; however, see Frank Dikötter, *Exotic Commodities: Modern Objects and Everyday Life in China,* New York: Columbia University Press, 2007.

# Index

point is that even weak
democratic, pluralist
countries — just need strong
enough to survive